A VANISHED SOCIETY

A VANISHED SOCIETY

ESSAYS IN

AMERICAN HISTORY

BY

ESTHER FELT BENTLEY

PRINCETON, NEW JERSEY

PRINCETON UNIVERSITY LIBRARY

1962

Published under the sponsorship of
Friends of the Princeton Library
with the assistance of
The Meriden Gravure Company
and Princeton University Press

Composition by Princeton University Press
Printing and collotypes by the Meriden Gravure Company
Design by P. J. Conkwright

CONTENTS

The essays published in this volume are reprinted from *The Princeton University Library Chronicle*; references to the issues of the *Chronicle* in which they originally appeared are given below.

ILLUSTRATIONS

following page 36

PHILIP ASHTON ROLLINS. Bronze plaque by Gutzon Borglum, 1902, bequeathed to Princeton University in 1957 by Mrs. Rollins.

KEOKUK'S SILVER PEACE MEDAL with its deerskin pouch, presented to the Princeton University Library in 1926 by Mrs. Archibald A. McLeod, in memory of her son, Archibald A. McLeod, Jr.

KEOKUK. Portrait in James O. Lewis, *The Aboriginal Port-Folio*, Philadelphia, 1835-[36], from the copy in the Princeton University Library.

WILLIAM L. DAYTON. Engraved portrait by J. C. Buttre after a photograph by Mathew Brady, from an impression in the Princeton University Library.

PRESIDENT MACLEAN introduces a fellow-alumnus. Autograph letter written by John Maclean to William L. Dayton, Princeton, December 2, 1862, introducing Charles Beasten, Jr., of the Class of 1861, from the Dayton Papers, presented to the Princeton University Library in 1953 by A. Dayton Oliphant.

ANNOUNCEMENT of the death of William L. Dayton, addressed to Mr. and Mrs. James B. Dayton, from the Dayton Papers.

PAGE 7 OF SAMUEL L. SOUTHARD'S LETTER on William Pinkney. Autograph draft in the Southard Papers, acquired by the Princeton University Library in 1957 through the generosity of Peter H. B. Frelinghuysen, Carl Otto v. Kienbusch, Sterling Morton, and Albert Southard Wright.

SAMUEL LEWIS SOUTHARD. Lithograph by E. B. & E. C. Kellogg after a portrait in silhouette by William H. Brown (William H. Brown, *Portrait Gallery of Distinguished American Citizens*, Hartford, 1845), from an impression in the Princeton University Library.

ix

FOREWORD

⁖ᕯ BOXFULS of old letters and relics are, in fine, boxfuls of ghosts and echoes, a swarm of apparitions and reverberations as dense as any set free by the lifted lid of Pandora. The interest is exquisite—when it is not intolerable—though doubtless an interest always, and even at the best, more easy to feel than to communicate.

. . . I am moved further to observe, I should still not have been able to resist the charm working in the words by which I come nearest to the character of my boxful. "A vanished society" is a label before which, wherever it be applied, the man of imagination must inevitably pause and muse. It is, for any bundle of documents, the most touching title in the world, and has only to be fairly legible to shed by itself a grace.

THESE reflections of Henry James upon the charm of "old letters and relics" were copied by Esther Bentley from his *William Wetmore Story and His Friends* and left with some notes she was assembling shortly before her death on December 8, 1961. During those last months of illness, in which her spirit and even her gaiety were undimmed, she was engaged in organizing and calendaring the last of a number of manuscript collections upon which she worked as Assistant Curator of Manuscripts in the Princeton University Library.

Her experience in studying and interpreting old manuscripts was a rich one. As research assistant to her distinguished husband, Gerald Eades Bentley, Murray Professor of English Literature at Princeton University, she worked beside him in the Public Record Office and most of the great libraries of the English-speaking world in the preparation of his studies of the theatrical history of sixteenth- and seventeenth-century England, most notably his monumental seven-volume *The Jacobean and Caroline Stage*. Her precise scholarship and her alert intellect combined with her broad experience to equip her admirably for the important but unheralded work of arranging and annotating a mass of manuscripts so that they would be of the greatest utility to other scholars.

Her intellectual curiosity, her warm human sympathy, and her gaiety of spirit inevitably led her to do more than merely organize collections. They enabled her to feel the exquisite interest in the material under her hands and to do what is more difficult, as James points out, to communicate that interest. Thus from time to time she contributed to *The Princeton University Library Chronicle* essays which give engaging glimpses of a vanished society.

I am proud to present on behalf of the Friends of the Princeton Library and as a tribute to Esther Bentley, this little volume of her essays in American history, collected from her contributions to the *Chronicle* under the title which she might have given them, *A Vanished Society*. They suggest that scholarship need not be dull, that history is made by human beings, and that sympathy and sensibility can blow away the dust of manuscript files.

WILLIAM S. DIX

A VANISHED SOCIETY

A Conversation with Mr. Rollins

"You must understand," said Mr. Rollins with a little smile as he reached for a cigarette, "that I'm sentimental about the cowboy. I have a right to be—I had my life saved three times by cowboys when I was just a kid."

He paused to see that his guest had suitable refreshment, made appropriate comments on the doctor's ruling which forbade his participation, and leaned back in his chair. He is a tall spare man ("Too tall to ride a bucking horse; my head described such a wide arc that I got dizzy before I ought to."), with white hair, keen, gentle blue eyes, and the generous brow and good bony structure of the face that Gutzon Borglum felt so beautifully in the head he did of Rollins and which Mrs. Rollins has presented to the University, along with the portrait by John Young-Hunter. The accidents of time and circumstance which so shaped his career that Princeton is proud to have his likeness on canvas and in bronze and is honored to receive the fruit of that career began their course when Philip Rollins was very young indeed, and are perhaps nowhere more dramatic than in the episodes which he mentioned so casually. Upon being pressed for details, Mr. Rollins said quickly, "You're sure this won't bore you? Well, once when I was riding herd in Montana, my horse went over a steep bank into quicksand —I was twelve then. He began to flounder as he was rapidly sucked down, but before I had time to do anything or to think of doing anything, I was pushed or thrown onto solid ground where the other riders could get a lariat to me and pull me up. That was all I knew at the moment. What had happened was that a cowboy had seen me go over the bank and had instantly spurred his own horse down into the quicksand beside me so that he could throw me with one powerful shove out of the saddle to safety. We never did find his body, though we waited for three days. Years later—I was afraid to say anything before then—I spoke to his brother about it. 'Why, hell,' he said, 'you got no call to worry. Nothing else he could do. He *had* to do that or leave the range.'

"Another time I was riding a horse that was too much for me. He threw me out of the saddle, but my foot caught in the stirrup, and I was in instant danger of being crushed by the hooves of the excited, bucking horse when I saw a flash of steel: a cowboy dived out of his saddle at my horse, grabbed hold of the stirrup, and with his open knife cut it loose. They told me that horse stamped on his head ten times before it could be stopped. The cowboy had known it was certain death to try to cut off the stirrup, but that didn't stop him. I was twelve then, too.

"The third time was in a blizzard in Montana. A blizzard could cause the loss of a whole valuable herd if it caught them in an unsuitable place, so when a bad storm came up the cattle had to be driven to a place where they would be out of drifts, preferably a low hill where the snow would be blown away so they could get to the grass but protected by higher hills from the full force of the wind. This night the wind was blowing in great wild gusts, driving and whipping the snow, which fell so thick that it was impossible to see more than a foot or so. It was a sudden and dangerous storm, and the cowboy who went out to try to head the lead steer into a safe spot told me not to come with him. I followed him anyway. Presently my horse stumbled, and I was thrown out of the saddle. When they found me next morning, I was lying on top of a steer that had been killed to provide me with warmth, and over me was not only my own bearskin coat but the cowboy's. Beside me was a lump of ice—the cowboy. Later on in the bunkhouse they brought me his saddle—it was the custom when a cowboy died to give his saddle to his best friend. I broke down then, but one of the men said, 'Don't cry, kid. He was ridin' for the brand.'

"That was the important thing—riding for the brand. It meant the same thing to them as dying for dear old Rutgers does to a college man, only it was a great deal more serious with them. They all had a strong pride in their vocation: it wasn't conceit, it was pride. They were as proud of being cowboys as those newly created cardinals over in Rome are of being cardinals. They were fiercely loyal to and proud of the ranch they worked for and willing to make any sacrifice for it, and they all believed in and obeyed the law of the country that any man, any stranger, would be protected against danger of whatever sort by the outfit of the ranch he was on.

"Riding for the brand was their whole life, and they were brought up in the tradition. Most of them were born on ranches, went from their cradles to a horse's back, and started in as professional cowboys when they were fifteen or sixteen, sometimes earlier. They had to be tough physically, they had to be loyal, and they had to be intelligent in the ways of the range, for sometimes

4

the safety of a herd of 30,000 cattle would depend on them. But, contrary to the current folklore, they weren't tough characters, ready to draw a gun at the slightest provocation. As a matter of fact, they seldom used their guns, in spite of what the movies show you. For one thing, ammunition was too expensive to waste. They always carried guns on the range, because they might find a wounded steer, or a wolf or a coyote, and there was always the theoretical danger of seeing a man-killing horse. (As a matter of fact, there weren't many man-killing horses; I saw only one in all the time I spent in the West.) Guns weren't toys to make a noise with; they were taken seriously, and there was a strict etiquette about their use. For instance, it was bad form to take a gun into the house; a cowboy riding up to visit at a ranch house would never wear his gun inside; he'd take it out of his holster and tie it to the horn of his saddle. Nobody ever had a gun on in the house unless he was getting ready to go out on the range. And it was anathema to touch another man's gun. Even as a ranch owner I would never have thought of picking up a cowboy's gun without first asking his permission."

Philip Ashton Rollins through his contact with ranching when it was at its apogee developed the love for the West and the interest in its customs and lore which led to his making the splendid collection of Western Americana which he and Mrs. Rollins have generously presented to Princeton. He is an Eastern man with an Eastern education, and the early auspices were that his experience would be confined to a small part of the Atlantic seaboard. At the time of his birth, January 20, 1869, his father was Commissioner of Internal Revenue under Johnson, but so that he might be born in New Hampshire his mother left Washington and went back to the family home in the little town of Great Falls, now Somersworth, just outside Dover. He was early introduced to learning, for he began Latin when he was not quite five, and Greek when he was not quite eight, and he is firmly convinced that no man can write well who has not known those languages. With a half year or so to go before he turns eighty, Rollins' own speech is the clear, fluent, diversified speech of one who early learned to shape a sentence and to respect a paragraph. The amazing thing, however, is the flow of stories, of facts; in the quiet room on Library Place, the pleasant, even voice creates a whole vanished world, a way of life now gone, a profession eliminated. In spite of his quizzical disclaimer, there is sentiment but not sentimentality in the stories, and if the ap-

5

praisals may sometimes be too generous, it is because the man is generous. Mr. Rollins was not a cowboy, but he has shared the cowboy's life; he observed it and appreciated it with the intensity of a boy, and he has increased his knowledge of its ways with the intelligence and assiduousness of a man.

Young Philip's formal education had two backgrounds, for during the winters of his boyhood he attended the West Philadelphia Academy and in the summers he went to a school in Wakefield, New Hampshire. It was at the latter school that he received a prejudice against the state of New Jersey that, he says, "I have never been able to outgrow. My teacher was from Harvard, and he taught us that during the French and Indian Wars when Massachusetts sent to New Jersey for help, New Jersey promised assistance but never sent it; that during the Revolution not only were there many Tories in New Jersey and none or few in Massachusetts, but that a commission from New Jersey which went to New York to buy supplies for the Colonial forces instead bought supplies for New Jersey; that in the War of 1812 Massachusetts' shipping suffered great losses while New Jersey was very little affected; and that finally in the Civil War Massachusetts furnished many soldiers, New Jersey comparatively few. I'm not saying, mind you, that this is strictly true, but it's what he taught us to believe as fact. Indeed, we had to learn the states of the Union from a wall map out of which New Jersey had been cut!"

The pattern which would have made Rollins a typical Easterner was broken by a bank failure and the great thrust westward by the railroads. In 1873 his father moved to Philadelphia as a partner in the great private banking firm of Jay Cooke and Company, the J. Pierpont Morgan Company of its time. The day he arrived Jay Cooke and Company failed. Mr. Rollins senior was appointed receiver and so was brought in touch with the Pennsylvania Railroad, with one of whose directors he went West to join a surveying party and, becoming interested in the possibilities of the country, was soon the owner of three enormous ranches. "At one time in the 1870's," said Mr. Rollins, "my father owned in one ranch more land than was in the state of Massachusetts. It extended from Helena to the edge of what is now Glacier National Park. And in all his ranches he owned more than 90,000 head of cattle. My father was one of the first ranchers to offer his cowboys a share in the profits of his ranch. He always had the best cowboys, he never had any trouble on his ranch, and he refused to hire a cowboy who hadn't served a prison sentence. He figured that a man who got in jail in those free and open days was tough enough to handle any situation—and my father was an elder in the Presbyterian Church!"

Mr. Rollins senior went West yearly to look after his ranches, and he took young Philip, whose mother was an invalid, with him, accompanied by an English tutor named Bronson. Philip's first stay of any length was in 1875-1876, when he was six and seven, but at the ripe age of five he spent four months in Wyoming in the care of Jim Bridger, the celebrated plainsman and scout. Every year thereafter, until he entered Princeton in 1885, he went out to the West, twice making the long and arduous drive from Texas to Wyoming with a herd of 3,000 cattle. The riders who accompanied the herd had a heavy responsibility, for the slow-moving, stubborn, excitable herd represented a tremendous investment and a potentially large profit, both of which could be lost through bad judgment, failure to check or prevent a stampede, or failure to recognize the warnings of sudden disaster. Indians had ceased to be a significant menace, but flash floods, freak blizzards, or the sudden drying up of water holes were dangers always threatening. It is worth noting that the cowboys to whose seasoned judgment was entrusted the job of moving capital worth $100,000 some 1500 miles from the bottom of the country to the top were seldom out of their twenties and often were no more than fifteen or sixteen. No outfit about to start out on the annual trek ever advertised in the Abilene paper for guest riders who would be coddled on the trip and introduced to a fine stretch of geography for a generous consideration, and we can be reasonably sure that Mr. Rollins went along not as a dude but as a working member, with his own string of horses and his full share of duties. Each cowboy had a string of about twelve horses which he rode two a day on slow days when there were no stampedes or other excitement or exertion to tire or lame the horses. They were never fed en route, but foraged for themselves; in fact, even on the ranches only the work (i.e., wagon) horses were ever fed, and even in the winter when the water holes and streams were frozen over they were not watered, for, according to Mr. Rollins, both horses and cattle, unlike human beings, can slake their thirst with snow.

Even college life did not break the ties with the Western ranges, for Mr. Rollins went back twice while he was an undergraduate, and in 1889, just after graduating, he went to Oregon as official photographer with a paleontological expedition under the direction of William Berryman Scott, the distinguished paleontologist. "We brought back," says Rollins, "a good many fossils, but they were mostly destroyed in a fire afterwards." After his return from the Princeton Expedition, he was in New York for a few months, then back to the West for not quite a year, and in 1894 he returned to his own ranch for the last time to sell his property to a Scotch syndicate. Two days after the sale, a sudden snow storm killed the herd and wiped out the syndicate. In those days men made fortunes and lost them in the cattle industry as they had before in mining and were to do later in oil.

But though he was no longer a ranch owner, Rollins made almost yearly trips to the West, in spite of the fact that he had settled down to the study of law, first at Columbia and then at New York University. He was admitted to the New York bar in 1895 and decided not to take the school examination for a degree. "A New York law school degree, at that time," he wrote in answer to an inquiry made later by the statistics-gathering Secretary of the University, "ranked with chicken pox." After being admitted to the bar, he became a member of the firm of Rollins and Rollins. The trips West, now that business no longer called him out, gradually became scouting expeditions of a different order, for his long and close association with the West of vast ranches, enormous herds, and especially with the particular kind of man which the cowboy had to be, led Rollins to begin to collect books and other more ephemeral material on the history of the country and of the industry which dominated that vast ungoverned empire. In his collecting and later in the painstaking and difficult job of classifying and cataloguing, he was enthusiastically joined by his wife, the former Beulah Brewster Pack, of Princeton, to whom he was married May 16, 1895.

It was, however, Professor Scott, his former teacher and great friend, who gave purpose and direction to the collecting activities. That Scott should have entered his life at all was a mistake, for Rollins' contact with the paleontologist came about through the mistaken impression that he was signing up for a "gut" course. Though the professor, a scant ten years older than the student, turned out to be a slave-driver, he was also an inspiring and illuminating teacher and a man of delightful humor, and he had a great influence in shaping Rollins' career, though not in the direction of paleontology, in which he made the briefest of starts. After Rollins' graduation from Princeton, Scott arranged for him to work with Julian Huxley, but after a fortnight in London, he was lured away on a big-game hunting expedition in Siberia, from which he went to Alaska on a scientific-sporting hunt of the grizzly bear. Paleontology even as a semi-serious pursuit was then put aside in favor of the law. The great teacher, however, is forever trying to shape and to mold, and after Rollins had become really serious in collecting Western Americana, Scott said to him, "Look here, Princeton lavished a lot of care and attention on you, and you gave us a lot of trouble. Now you ought to make some return. Don't be just a dilettante collector—make a study of your material and write a really accurate scientific study of that world before all the evidence is gone." The result was that Rollins commenced author with *The Cowboy; His Characteristics, His Equipment, and His Part in the Development of the West*, whose title gives a clear indication of the scope and sober, fact-displaying intent of the author. It was published in 1922, and a revised and enlarged edition was brought out in 1936, providing within its covers material for all future writers and lovers of the West. The versatility of the author is demonstrated by the later publication on the one hand of two books for boys which Scribner's wisely persuaded him to write, which small boys dote on and parents cheerfully read aloud over and over again, and on the other of his edition of Robert Stuart's account of an overland trip in 1812-1813 which received columns and columns of respectful and delighted reviews and which caused one distinguished historian to say, "The biographical note on Stuart's career, the foreword, and the mass of notes which accompany each chapter, are models of scholarly work, making easy the task of historians of the West who consult the volume." Another concluded five columns of review: "Not only has Mr. Rollins brought to light one of the most important and absorbing records of early Western exploration, but, in editing this volume with such painstaking care after exhaustive examinations of available sources, he has also presented an example of American historical research scholarship at its best. The volume is beyond praise."

One unexpected bit of glory came to Mr. Rollins as the result of the publication of *The Cowboy*, for at the Pendleton Round-up in 1923 the liveliest bucking horse in the camp was named Philip Rollins. On the back of a picture postcard of the equine Philip Rollins about to unseat a grimly clutching rider with a fine, high sidewise swing, Mr. Rollins wrote to a friend, "If, by writing a history of the Cowboy, one has a bucking horse named for him, why not write a history of royalty and be awarded four queens? They would be grand in a poker game." The Pendleton Round-up that year was designed to honor him, and as Mr. Rollins as guest of honor trotted around past the stands with the officials, a band of twenty-one cowboys rode up to him, swept off their hats, and threw them on the ground. It was the equivalent of a twenty-one gun salute. "What did you do?" I asked. And he replied softly, "I bawled!"

It would be interesting to know which he prized more, that dramatic tribute or the Litt.D. conferred on him by Princeton the following year, partly for his work in recording the history and habits of the cowboy. His citation, written by Dean West, begins: "His success in the law and in highly confidential war service have figured less in public view than his marvelous skill in showing that the making and blending of the West from the Missouri River to the California Mountains was largely done by the much misprized cowboys, that virile race of tireless horsemen now vanishing." Though the prose of degree citations is perhaps always a trifle lush, still the fact is that "his writings are the first to disclose in just proportions, larger and lesser, what manner of men they were and the strong part they played, to take them out of the false lights of melodrama and place them in the sunlight of fact, and to make them real and more really romantic."

In our times the cowboy has become the symbol of a wild, free, independent life, but, according to Mr. Rollins, the shooting daredevil had no place in the serious business of ranching. The life was often lonely, and the responsibilities heavy. When the cowboy went to town—and from the outlying ranches that would be only twice a year, after being paid off—his first action was always a very prosaic one: he headed straight for the barber shop for a shave and a haircut. "Perhaps one of the reasons for the haircut," said Mr. Rollins, "was that often in those days horse thieves when caught had the tops of their ears cut off, so they wore their hair long to hide the deformity. Of course if there was a lady to be impressed, there was quite a bit of effort expended. I've seen cowboys, the night before going to town, sit up for hours polishing every part of their guns; they seemed to think that a well polished gun had just as much effect on the female heart as the soldier used to believe his sword did."

After the barber shop the cowboy usually went right off to the gambling houses. Some, of course, went to houses of ill-fame, but very few; it was gambling that drew them. "I've seen a man put down six months' wages—the average rider made twenty dollars a month, a foreman forty dollars—on one turn of the roulette wheel, and lose it all, say 'Oh, hell!' and start back for the ranch, looking forward to returning to town in six months."

If he went to a saloon, he followed a strict order of precedence in entering or leaving. At the top of the list were ranch owners and foremen, Indian scouts, government scouts, and stage coach drivers, then the riders in the order of the importance of their ranches. This order was punctiliously followed. The cowboy was fundamentally a very serious man; he kept up his courage by pretending to be flippant and affected a carelessness he didn't really feel.

"But he had more sense than to dress like the gaudy acrobats in the Western movies and present-day so-called rodeos. From Texas to Oregon the cowboy eschewed bright colors in his dress that would make him conspicuous on the range; the neckerchief was not a brilliant thing gaily streaming behind, nor was it worn, as one solemn historian reported, to protect the neck from sunburning, but was a sober square knotted in back so that it could be quickly pulled up over the mouth and nose when the cowboy had to ride into the clouds of dust stirred up by the herd. The broad brimmed hat was worn not for dash but to keep out the broiling sun and the infrequent rain; on the ranches of the Northwest the brim was narrower because of the snow in the winter months. As a matter of fact, the cowboy had very little gear and very little to spend money on. A hat was a life-time purchase; so, except for accidents, of course, were his boots, chaparajos, saddle, and lariat.

"Another difference in the equipment of the Northwest and the Southwest was to be seen in the lariat. In the Northwest the lariat was most frequently made of rawhide cunningly braided, while in the Texas area it was made of sisal grass. In the early days they were all made of rawhide, of course, but when sisal grass was developed in Texas it was discovered that it made lariats that were both stronger and lighter. On the Northern ranches the lariat was usually sixty feet long, on the Texas ranches seventy feet. The Texas cowboy had a curious custom of fastening the home end of his lariat around his saddle horn before he threw, while the Northern rider snubbed his around the horn while the noose was in the air. Those men were artists with the lariat. Throwing it, whether on foot or on horseback, demanded rhythm, balance, and a sense of timing exquisite and instinctive. As little kids they played with lariats, as boys now play with balls, until they knew how and when to throw without conscious thought. And they were good: they had to be. It is estimated that a 1200-pound steer makes a pull of a ton and a half on a lariat—that's the reason for the high heels, of course, to dig into the ground or brace against the stirrup—and I've seen a steer when caught just right about the neck jerked into the air and thrown in a wide arc.

"The saddles differed considerably too in the two parts of the West. The Texas saddles were narrower and had more dip; the Montana ones were flatter, due to the difference in horses in the two regions. The reasons for that difference are interesting. The horse, of course, was originally brought to this continent by the Spaniards. The men who cared for and guarded the horses were lazy and careless, with the result that many of them escaped, and many also were stolen by the Indians. Increasing in number, they worked their way up the country in a Y-pattern, with a short prong into Texas and a long prong into Oregon. In Texas, where there was little water and sparse vegetation, they had to exercise a lot to get enough to eat, and as the years went by and generation succeeded generation, the Texas mustang developed, a lean, rangy, tough little animal. In Oregon, on the other hand, where there was an adequate rainfall and lush pastures, the development was into a bigger, heavier horse which needed a bigger, flatter saddle. The Montana saddle also had a double cinch where the Texas had a single one.

"There are practically no saddle catalogues extant now to show us these differences. They got worn out, and anyway such things weren't kept. Some years ago I went to a saddle man I knew in Wyoming and asked him if he had any old saddle catalogues for my collection. 'That's a funny thing,' he said. 'A fellow from Harvard was here just last week and said he'd give me fifty dollars for every catalogue I could get him over fifteen years old. Tell you what—since you're a Princeton man and collecting for the Princeton Library, I'll just *give* you the whole lot.' As a matter of fact, he did better than that: he sent a circular letter to all the likely people he knew and so got me a lot more.

"There are practically no account books left from those early ranches, either. Very few were kept; in fact no big enterprise was probably ever so unsystematically run. All the ranchers figured that the calves were all clear profit, and after they were sold all the records were destroyed.

"I ran across something recently that is even more rare and that I thought I had lost—an undesirable's notice, one of the last I ever saw. Whenever anybody came onto the range who wasn't wanted, the Ranchers Association got out a printed notice which said in effect, 'It has come to the notice of the Association that the following people have been seen in this vicinity. Anybody hearing of them or seeing them, please notify a member of the Association.' Sounds innocent enough, but it was really a notice to get rid of the people named, get them out of the country. There were about twenty-five members of the Association, who distributed the leaflets at their discretion. The Association also employed range detectives, who were hired to do a job and no inquiries made as to their methods. Their reports were almost always a brief note on the successful completion of a task; no details were given. I remember that at one time out of fourteen range detectives twelve were Texans.

"As a matter of fact, the good cowboys were apt to be Texans. To be sure, the average cowboy could sit on anything short of a windmill, but even so the Texans were better riders, knew more about cattle, were very much better lariat throwers. And they were proud—proud of their skill and proud of being Texans. Somebody ought to do a study of why they were so violently and peculiarly proud of being Texans. It had nothing to do with the size of the state, though of course they were proud of that. I'm not a Texan myself, but I've ridden the range with a lot of them, and I never had the nerve to ask them the source of their pride. And once a Texan, always a Texan, no matter how long they had been away or how far. Why, I've seen half-a-dozen cowboys sitting on their spurs argue for hours that five rowels was the only right number for spurs. There are five points in the Texas star, you see.

"All cowboys would argue indefinitely; it was their chief source of entertainment. There was a rule that you couldn't change sides more than three times in the course of one argument, just to keep some kind of order. Some of them were excellent dialecticians. The favorite topic was religion, particularly the creation of the world. The essential virtues for them were courage in a man and daintiness and decency in a woman.

13

"One striking fact about the development of the West which I think we are apt to forget is that almost all the ranchmen in Montana and Wyoming had English partners. They were mostly remittance men sent over by their families for a few years until a scandal had been forgotten, or younger sons. They seldom stayed more than two or three years; the scandals blew over, or they came into the title, or because of a death came closer to it, and so they went home. But they brought a lot of money into the West; some years ago I tried to find out how much they brought and how much they lost—most of it was lost—but I never did get any conclusive figures. The Associated Scottish Banks after working on it for me for a year gave it up because it was too difficult to get hold of enough definite facts.

"The Englishmen also brought a lot of culture into the West. There were practically no books out there, but an Englishman always brought Shakespeare with him: it was the decent thing to do. And they read their books, too, read them aloud to the cowboys, many of whom never got any farther in their schooling than the rudiments of reading and writing. I've seen a bunch of cowboys sitting on their spurs listening with absolute silence and concentration while somebody read aloud. They were discriminating too, even if they lacked the sophisticated vocabulary of formal criticism. Once when something of Oscar Wilde's was being read, one of the cowboys got up and left the room. Later I asked him why, and he said, 'I don't see no beauty in watching a hog eat swill.' And I remember once after we'd been listening to *Julius Caesar*, one of them said to me, 'That Shakespeare is the only poet I've ever heard who was fed on raw meat.' When I sold my ranch in Montana I divided my books among the riders, and eighteen out of twenty-one wanted Shakespeare. I sent out fifteen sets of Shakespeare that year!

"I'll tell you a funny little story about the cowboy and his appreciation of culture. Years after I had bought so many copies of Shakespeare, Mrs. Rollins and I were in Venice when Buffalo Bill's show was playing in Verona. One morning I was near the Hospital of St. Mark, near which stands the colossal equestrian statue of Colleoni, and I went to see once more that magnificent pair, the noble spirited horse and the easy, bold, confident rider. I found a cowboy there standing stock-still before the statue. A gendarme saw me watching him and came up to ask if the man were dangerous; said he'd been there every morning for a week staring at the statue. 'No,' I said, 'he's not dangerous; I know him.' So I went up and spoke to him. He turned and greeted me and then said, with the greatest reverence in his voice, 'That ain't a statue to no one man—that's a statue to a whole damn nation!' "

The Madison Medal and Chief Keokuk

FROM early colonial times it was the custom of the Spanish, the French, and the English alike to give medals to Indian chiefs upon the conclusion of a treaty or to signalize other important occasions. Amongst the materials being readied for the French expedition to America in 1780 under Rochambeau we find striped blankets, silver arm bands, and silver medals with the French royal arms. These were necessary, it was said, "à ranimer l'amour des sauvages pour les Français."

When the thirteen colonies became welded into the United States, the new government at once set about to have medals of its own, not only to distribute upon appropriate occasions but also to give to the Indian leaders in exchange for the ones bestowed on them by other governments. Since possession of a medal betokened acknowledgment of loyalty and allegiance to the country issuing it, it was expedient to gather in as many as possible of the medals given by the French and English.[1]

The Indian chiefs on their part regarded their medals highly, wearing them on ceremonial occasions, "with as much pride, and as much propriety, as the orders of nobility which decorate the nobles of Europe."[2] They were passed down from father to son,

[1] The chief sources consulted on these medals are Bauman L. Belden, *Indian Peace Medals Issued in the United States*, New York, The American Numismatic Society, 1927, and J. F. Loubat, *The Medallic History of the United States of America, 1776-1876*, New York, 1878.

[2] Thomas Loraine McKenney and James Hall, *History of the Indian Tribes of North America, with Biographical Sketches and Anecdotes of The Principal Chiefs. Embellished with One Hundred and Twenty Portraits, from the Indian Gallery in the Department of War, at Washington*, I, 74. The three folio volumes of this work (Sabin 43410a) were published separately in Philadelphia, the first in 1836, the second in 1838, and the third in 1844. McKenney (1785-1859) was superintendent of Indian trade from 1816 to 1822 and director of the bureau of Indian affairs from 1824 to 1830. Hall (1793-1868), who wrote most of the text, was an author, lawyer, and banker whose accounts of pioneer life in the Ohio valley and Illinois are valuable source books of history and legend.

The portraits accompanying the biographies were exactly copied and colored from the paintings in the Indian Gallery of the War Department. Eventually these paintings were moved to a wing of the Smithsonian which burned in 1865 and very few of the portraits were saved, so that the lithographic reproductions in McKenney and Hall have preserved the lineaments and costumes of men whose kind have vanished.

or from chief to chief, frequently serving as the distinguishing mark of a new chief. Because they represented the constant effort of the government to establish firm and friendly relations with the Indian nations in a period of rapid flux and change, they came to be known as Indian Peace medals.

The earliest medals issued by the young United States were more the product of the jeweler's art than of the medalist's, being individually made and hand-engraved. The first of this type bears the date 1789, the year that Washington was inaugurated; it is engraved, rather inexpertly, on a thin sheet of silver, oval in shape, and only two examples were known to Belden. The first of the cast medals were dated 1796, though they were not delivered from England until 1798.[3]

It was not until 1801 that Indian Peace medals were struck at the United States Mint in Philadelphia, but from that time new medals were issued for each president. The 1801 Jefferson medal was designed by John or Johann Mathias Reich (1768-1833), a German diesinker and medalist who had been brought over as assistant to the chief engraver at the Mint. It bears a profile portrait of Jefferson on the obverse side and on the reverse a tomahawk crossed with a calumet or peace pipe above clasped hands, and the words "Peace and Friendship" in three lines. This general design—a profile portrait of the current president on the obverse and the peace-and-friendship motif on the reverse—was followed with slight modification for all medals through the administration of Zachary Taylor; thereafter the design of the reverse was altered. An entry in the journal of the Lewis and Clark expedition for August 17, 1805, illustrates the use and distribution of medals:

> We then distributed our presents: to Cameahwait we gave a medal of the small size, with the likeness of president Jefferson. and on the reverse a figure of hands clasped with a pipe and tomahawk: to this was added an uniform coat, a shirt, a pair of scarlet leggings, a carrot ot tobacco, and some small articles. Each of the other chiefs received a small medal struck during the presidency of general Washington, a shirt, handkerchief, leggings, a knife, and some tobacco. Medals of the same sort were also presented to two young warriors, who

[3] Belden, *Indian Peace Medals*, pp. 6, 22-24.

though not chiefs were promising youths and very much respected in the tribe.[4]

For a hundred years, from 1789 to 1889, Indian Peace medals were made and distributed to the sachems of the tribes and nations occupying land into which the white men were more and more rapidly moving, but relatively few of them have come into collections. Copies in bronze of all these medals have been made and sold at the Philadelphia Mint, and those of the later presidents— Grant through Harrison—are still available. Princeton University Library has an almost complete run of these copies, as well as two original medals. These originals are both, appropriately enough, from the administration of James Madison, the first Princeton graduate to become president of the United States. One is of bronze, 5 cm. in diameter and .4 cm. thick; the other is of silver, 5.1 cm. in diameter, .2 cm. thick.

The silver medal, somewhat rubbed and worn, together with a deerskin pouch (see Plate II), was given to the Library in 1926 by Mrs. Archibald A. McLeod, Sr., in memory of her son, Archibald A. McLeod, Jr., Class of 1906. Mrs. McLeod's father, Barton Atkins of Buffalo, while traveling in Montana in 1885 had obtained the medal from a cattle-herder who had found it in 1878 on the site of the Custer Massacre.

The medal was duly catalogued by the Library, it was even used in a recent exhibition, but its history had been lost sight of in the years since its acquisition until a letter from the president of the Lee County Historical Society of Keokuk, Iowa, prompted an inquiry, which disclosed the fact that according to legend this medal had once belonged to Chief Keokuk of the Sauk (or Saukie or Sac) and Fox nations.

Keokuk (*ca.* 1780-1848) was one of the most resourceful, accomplished, and eloquent chiefs of whom record has come down to us. He did not inherit his position as chief but achieved it by his gifts for daring, clever, and bold leadership. According to McKenney and Hall, he was "in all respects, a magnificent savage. Bold, enterprising, and impulsive, he is also politic, and possesses an intimate knowledge of human nature, and a tact which enables him to bring

[4] Paul Allen, ed., *History of the Expedition under the Command of Captains Lewis and Clark. . . . Performed during the Years 1804-5-6*, Philadelphia, 1814, I, 384.

the resources of his mind into prompt operation."[5] In person he was

a large and finely formed man. His manners are dignified and
graceful, and his elocution, as well in conversation as in public
speaking, highly energetic and animated. His flow of language
and rapidity of utterance are remarkable; yet his enunciation
is so clear and distinct, that it is said not a syllable is lost. His
voice is powerful and agreeable, and his countenance prepos-
sessing. It is not often that so fine a looking man is seen as this
forest chieftain, or one whose deportment is so uniformly correct.[6]

Keokuk displayed an astonishing sagacity and restraint in his
dealings with the white neighbors of his tribe and showed a natural
dignity and tact in his public appearances. These qualities and the
discipline which he was able to exercise over his people are evi-
denced in an account of a conference called in Washington in 1837.

The meeting took place in a church, at one end of which a
large stage was erected, while the spectators were permitted to
occupy the pews in the remainder of the house. The Secretary
[of War, Joel Poinsett], representing the President of the
United States, was seated on the centre of the stage, facing the
audience, the Sioux on his right hand, and the Sauks and
Foxes on his left, the whole forming a semicircle. These hos-
tile tribes presented in their appearance a remarkable contrast
—the Sioux appearing tricked out in blue coats, epaulettes,
fur hats, and various other articles of finery which had been
presented to them, and which were now incongruously worn
in conjunction with portions of their own proper costume—
while the Sauks and Foxes, with a commendable pride and
good taste, wore their national dress without any admixture,
and were studiously painted according to their own notions
of propriety. But the most striking object was Keokuk, who
sat at the head of his delegation, on their extreme left, facing
his mortal enemies, the Sioux, who occupied the opposite side
of the stage, having the spectators upon his left side, his own
people on his right, and beyond them the Secretary of War.
He sat . . . grasping in his right hand a war banner, the symbol

[5] McKenney and Hall, II, 71.
[6] *Ibid.*, II, 80.

of his station as ruling chief. His person was erect, and his eye fixed calmly but steadily upon the enemies of his people. On the floor, and leaning upon the knee of the chief, sat his son, a child of nine or ten years old, whose fragile figure and innocent countenance afforded a beautiful contrast to the athletic and warlike form, and the intellectual though weather-beaten features of Keokuk. The effect was in the highest degree picturesque and imposing.[7]

When the Sioux orators had finished their vehement and acrimonious harangues, Keokuk rose,

advanced to the Secretary, and having saluted him, returned to his place, which being at the front of the stage, and on one side of it, his face was not concealed from any of the several parties present. His interpreter stood beside him. The whole arrangement was judicious, and, though apparently unstudied, showed the tact of an orator. He stood erect, in an easy but martial posture, with his robe thrown over his left shoulder and arm, leaving the right arm bare, to be used in action. His voice was fine, his enunciation remarkably clear, distinct, and rapid. . . . He spoke with dignity, but with great animation, and some of his retorts were excellent. . . . "They tell you that peace has often been made, but that we have broken it. How happens it then that so many of their braves have been slain in our country? I will tell you. They invaded us—we never invaded them—none of my braves have been killed in their country. We have their scalps, and can tell where we took them."[8]

The eloquence of Keokuk at this conference prompted *Niles' National Register* on October 7, 1837, to call him "one of the most sagacious Indians on our frontier. . . . the Thersites of the day."

On an earlier occasion at the Prairie du Chien conference of August, 1825, Keokuk was also one of the principal actors. The portrait that is here reproduced (Plate III) was painted at Prairie du Chien by James Otto Lewis (1799-1858).[9] It can be seen that in

[7] *Ibid.*, II, 78.

[8] *Ibid.*, II, 79.

[9] Lewis painted more than seventy important or significant figures among the Indian tribes, traveling about the country and frequently attending the councils called by government officials. He published his portraits in parts in folio without

the portrait Keokuk is wearing an Indian Peace medal. He received at least two, for in the portrait that was painted of him with his son at the time of the later Washington conference both are wearing medals.

Chief Keokuk died in 1848 in Kansas, where his tribe had by this time been moved, but in 1883 his remains were brought back to the Iowa town that bears his name. Thirty years later a bronze statue of an Indian was erected on the stone monument containing the bones of the once-proud chief. It is ironical that the sculptor has given this figure the costume of the Sioux, the tribe that was the greatest enemy of Keokuk's own.

Although an unverifiable family tradition may not be a sufficient basis for claiming, with strict scholarly accuracy, that Princeton's silver medal bearing John Reich's portrait of Madison was the one actually presented to Chief Keokuk, it is nevertheless pleasant to be associated even in legend with the "magnificent savage," "the Thersites of the day."

---

text in 1835-36, probably in an attempt to anticipate the McKenney and Hall volumes, under the title *The Aboriginal Port-Folio* (Sabin 40812), of which the Library has two sets.

It is interesting to compare Lewis's portraits with those in the McKenney and Hall volumes in those cases where the same figures are treated. In the latter work the portraits are official, as it were; there is a smoothness about them, often a Europeanization of the features and a general blandness of expression which render them, interesting as they are, superficial and unrevealing. Lewis's work is cruder, but in its very crudeness there is a sense of immediacy, of particularity, and of unvarnished truthfulness that gives great credibility. Lewis was not a good enough painter to give life to his subjects, but he has left us portraits of such rough truthfulness that we can breathe life into them.

A portrait of Chief Keokuk painted by George Catlin in 1836 is in the University of Pennsylvania Museum, Philadelphia. Still another portrait of him by Charles Bird King, *ca.* 1830, is in the Redwood Library and Athenaeum, Newport, Rhode Island. Cf. Nos. 15 and 25 in the catalogue of the University of Pennsylvania Museum exhibition, *The Noble Savage, The American Indian in Art*, 8 May-8 September, 1958. The Catlin portrait is reproduced on the cover.

21

A Diplomat's Mailbag

William Lewis Dayton in Paris, 1861-1864

A COLLECTION of materials known as the William Lewis Dayton Papers, which was for some time on deposit in the Manuscripts Division of the Princeton University Library, was given to the Library in November of 1953 by A. Dayton Oliphant, Class of 1910, a Justice of the Supreme Court of New Jersey and a collateral descendant of Dayton.

The materials in the collection cluster around the figure of William Lewis Dayton, who was graduated from Princeton with the Class of 1825. He was born near Baskingridge, Somerset County, New Jersey, in 1807 and died in 1864 in Paris, where he had been United States Minister (the rank of ambassador not yet having been established) since the spring of 1861. The papers are largely from these years in France. They consist in the main of rough drafts or copies of letters sent by Mr. Dayton, letters received by him, including a large number of letters of introduction, legation and personal accounts, canceled checks, newspaper clippings (chiefly related to the famous "Trent" case and the engagement of the "Alabama" and the "Kearsarge"), and certain personal papers such as insurance, passports, estate matters, and the like. There is in addition a much smaller number of letters written to and by his son, William Lewis Dayton, Jr., Princeton Class of 1858, who served as assistant secretary in the legation in Paris during his father's lifetime and who was later himself Minister to The Hague, 1882-1885, together with a few papers concerning other members of the family.

Use was made of certain of these papers for the spring exhibition of 1956 called "Americans in Paris," of which it is perhaps worth while to mention the caricature by George Catlin of Napoleon III and the long and detailed letter written by William Lewis Dayton, Jr. to his father describing the engagement of the "Alabama" and the "Kearsarge," of which he was an eyewitness from the cliffs of Cherbourg.[1]

[1] See "Americans in Paris; Catalogue of an Exhibition, Princeton University Library, May 4-June 30, 1956," *The Princeton University Library Chronicle*, XVII, No. 4 (Summer, 1956), Nos. 97, 98, 99, 101, 103, 104, and reproduction of Catlin's caricature.

The following article is based on certain materials in the papers which are admittedly peripheral to their chief importance.

———————◆•◆———————

Among the papers of William Lewis Dayton there are a number of letters which illustrate piquantly the variety of problems that an ambassador must deal with in the midst of the pressing international crises that form the staple of his official life. The fact that Dayton was United States Minister to France during the troubled and bitter times of the Civil War meant that the difficulties and complexities of his office were increased in seriousness as well as in number, for Europe was warily eying the conflict across the Atlantic, her sympathies perhaps more than half engaged by the secessionist side. Dayton's duties, as we can abundantly see from his papers, were manifold. He had to procure arms for the United States and to try to prevent the secessionist states from getting them, or ships, or any other advantages; he had to gather in as much information as he could about European attitudes and sympathies and to try to disseminate as much as possible of favorable publicity for the North in order to influence these attitudes and sympathies; with little or no French and no previous experience of ambassadorial responsibilities and methods, he had to keep in touch on the one hand with the liberal antislavery group in France and on the other to combat the strongly secessionist sentiment which animated a perhaps larger group of influential men and to learn enough about them both to keep his own government fully informed—all this at a time when at the very least three weeks would elapse between the posting of a letter and a full response to it.

That Dayton was able to handle the difficult situation in which he at once found himself on arriving in Paris in the late spring of 1861 we can deduce from the comments of the Paris press at the time of his death in December, 1864. The *Constitutionnel* says that he was "one of the most distinguished and enlightened men of the United States" and speaks especially of his "courteous manner and his always well-chosen and measured language." The *Patrie*, though it supported the Confederate cause, regretted the death of "The able diplomatist, as well as honest man and perfect gentleman"; while the *Opinion Nationale* remarked that he "fulfilled his diplomatic functions with a rectitude and tact which procured him the esteem of even his political adversaries."

In the midst of the great problems which required Dayton's rectitude and tact, there were lesser ones also calling upon a courteous manner and well-chosen and measured language. The day's mail often brought much to distract, amuse, and annoy. There were, for instance, visiting compatriots, for Americans in surprising numbers continued to travel abroad, and a great many of them wished to be presented at court. The Minister had to vouch for these republican seekers of royal experience: "a young gentleman of education"; "a distinguished professor in a medical college of New York"; another "young gentleman of education travelling for improvement, when at home he is a student at law"; "a gentleman of fortune . . . [with] no profession or occupation"; "a gentleman of high respectability"; "Mr. Davis & his three daughters . . . . He is 'un rentier,' and his daughters of most presentable appearance."

The years go by, the war drags on, but still the Minister addresses M. le Baron with the recommendations: "a gentleman of fortune I believe & largely engaged in ships &c to India"; "a man of literary pursuits"; "a Banker of N. York city. He is a gentleman in appearance & manners"; "a lady in her appearance, social position & manners"; "a merchant retired from business, with a fortune largely increased as I am informed by recent operations in the silver mines of Nevada."

These minor duties, and such vexations as finding that a custom-built coach sent from home, though well-made and handsome, was much too small, must have seemed like pleasures when there came to hand certain letters not intended for Dayton but vitally interesting to him. They were written by the Confederate commissioner to England, James M. Mason, whose seizure on board the British mail-steamer "Trent," with John Slidell, the Confederate commissioner to France, threatened for a time to precipitate war between England and the United States. Mason was an experienced man, and it must have made Dayton squirm to read Mason's report not only that "Dayton has been received very coldly at the Department" but that "Dayton is being played with by Drouyn [the French Minister of Foreign Affairs]. I send you proofs of it." How simple the complexities of a law case in Trenton must have seemed to the Minister then!

There was always his family to provide distraction from state affairs. The eldest son, Ferdinand Van Der Veer Dayton, was an active participant in the Civil War; as a member of the Second New Jersey Cavalry he was appointed Surgeon-in-Chief of the

Southern District of Mississippi with headquarters at Natchez. In June of '62 he wrote from the Valley of the Shenandoah such a letter as would make for anxious thoughts, of a battle near Harrisonburg in which his regiment fell into an ambush. "Gen Bayards Brigade, that is ours, in fact our regiment of Buck tails, has done all the fighting & suffered all the loss. Out of our regiment there is about 140 fit for duty today . . . . I have had shells, round shot & musket balls as close to me as I ever want them to come again. Yesterday when I was trying to get up to the wounded a round shot just missed me and hit in the ground in front of my horse."

Later Ferdinand was hospitalized with diarrhea, which killed so many soldiers in the Civil War. A passage in the letter telling of his discharge from the hospital illustrates what now seems the peculiarly informal nature of war at that time. He hopes, he says, that his regiment is still in the place where it had been last reported to him, "although I heard last night from some ladies that were at Mrs Strattons that Gen Bayard had orders to have 12 days rations on hand which looks as if it were intended to move for a long Scout. I hope I shall catch them before they go. The Gen will not move if he can help it as he wants to be married on the 18th."

Dayton's other children were in France with him; his second son, William Lewis Dayton, Jr., was assistant secretary at the Ministry in Paris, and his daughter Annie kept Mrs. Dayton company on shopping expeditions (the bills from dressmakers and jewelers are full of interest). The youngest son, Edward, to whom Ferdinand in one letter enclosed "some Reb Postage Stamps that have never been used," at least for part of the time that Dayton was Minister was living as a pupil with a certain M. Jouancoux at Caderousse. In a letter to Dayton M. Jouancoux says that Edward is a good boy, "religieux, bon, complaisant, honnête," who works hard and speaks French pretty well; he has read all of ancient history and is good at arithmetic. "Malheureusement," says M. Jouancoux just at the point when a parent might commence to relax, "Malheureusement sa mémoire ayant été peu cultivée dans l'enfance, il n'a pu retenir tout ce qu'il a appris." In the 1860's it was not John Dewey who could be blamed! Perhaps the clue to Eddie's trouble lies in M. Jouancoux's later comment: "Au reste, il n'a pas un goût bien fort pour les choses littéraires; c'est un esprit essentiellement positif. Il ferait un bon *gentleman farmer*: il aime beaucoup la campagne; il s'y porte

25

bien et tout ce qui concerne l'agriculture et le jardinage l'inté-
resse beaucoup."

One wonders if this "esprit positif" ever heard from his father
anything about becoming a gentleman farmer; whether his literary interests increased after a little prodding, whether his memory was jogged by a reduction in allowance. In a letter to his
mother Eddie says bleakly that "M^r J thinks Frank [another pupil]
will get along in life but he has not much hope for Eddie." The
rest of the letter is cheerful and affectionate, and in a later one
it is pleasing to observe that the putative gentleman farmer has
enough "esprit positif" to request ten francs for a pair of slippers;
"you know I bought a cheap pair in Paris but they were not worth
a snap . . . I think I have spent almost as much money for shoes
(mending) as for all other things since I have been here, the
slippers cost 9^f so that 10^f will be enough."

The Minister had scarcely settled the new carpets from England on the floors of the apartment at Rue Jean Goujon No. 17
when he received a crackling letter from Eliza W. Gen. Having,
she says, all her life "received the highest attentions from the
highest people and when in Washington being visited not only
by the President himself by Miss Lane the members of the Cabinet and their ladies, but those also most highly esteemed in our
own party many times, I very naturally supposed that my call
upon Mrs. Dayton would be returned (or noticed at least)."
Her son, in America, "being justly indignant," Mrs. Gen says,
procured her a letter of introduction from Boston, where he was
informed that "Mrs. Monroe had said thus-and-so to Mrs. Dayton,
and he presumed, *therefore*, she had not called." Since gossip
is entrancing no matter what the year, one longs to hear that
"thus-and-so," but though Mrs. Gen does not repeat what information was presumably passed on to Mrs. Dayton, she oblig-
ingly gives us some tidbits to mull over. After a few tossings of
the head over Mrs. Monroe, she says, "Permit me to add that
I never 'asked' Mr M for money—I went *afterwards* to *hire*, on
good security—Mr Gen never asked for money at all, in any
way—he was *requested by Mr M. through me 'to call.' "

Mrs. Gen then draws a deep breath and continues. "The reason
I went to hire money in lieu of him, was, that being newly married and having my own and the daughter of a friend with me,
I did not wish *so soon*, to trouble my husband for '*pin-money*'—
and the more especially as having been absent from Paris some

years, it took some time to arrange his business affairs—and my own property in Mass^tts . . . is temporarily embarrassed."

Mrs. Gen's affairs are so fascinatingly involved that one is grateful to her for putting at least an outline down on paper, and her movement from point to point is extremely skillful. Note below how explanation of a damning criticism moves into triumphant justification and thence into what, if one did not feel delicate in the presence of a lady so sensitive to slights, might be called bribery. She says:

> The "sanguine feeling in the management of my affairs" to which Mr Hall alludes, is the expensive manner in which I established the Seminary of which I transmit the Catalogue and which I am happy to state was a *perfect success*. I was summoned from it at the printed invitation of clergymen of six denominations residing in Washington [a shrewd thrust!] and should have been equally successful there had I remained, but was advised by political friends *of what has occurred there*, & discontinued.
>
> As I wrote, I am well known to those most highly esteemed in the administration party, but, (with *many others*), I never admired Mr. Burlingame, and never invited him to my receptions—I fancy he does not admire me!
>
> Hon. W^m. Appleton of Boston, the Govenor [*sic*] of Mass. the Mayor of Boston (my native place) and many others there, gave me flattering letters of introduction.
>
> I have troubled you with all this, My dear Sir, because in the coming political movements and consequent changes foreshadowed to me privately by friends at Washington, I shall, if I have your friendship, write & speak in a manner more gratifying to all concerned, and so will my son (who is telegraphic correspondent of the New York Times) and be able thus to return your kindness perhaps.

After the divagations and complications of Mrs. Gen's letter it must have been a pleasure to Mr. Dayton to plunge into correspondence with Charles Francis Adams, United States Minister in London, on the sound and straightforward subject of procuring arms for the prosecution of the war.

Another kind of responsibility was laid upon the Minister by a Mrs. Francis Peters, writing from the Hôtel Monnet (with three crowns) at Vevey. After establishing her family position in Jefferson County, Virginia, she says that in her "present unprotected position" she has selected Mr. Dayton as "the one most competent to receive papers which the *Duc de Medumn* may probably place in your hands as proofs of his rank and serious intention of offering himself to my daughter. . . . Suffice to say that the Duc is a man of about 23 years of age holding the rank of Major in the service of the King of Italy. He is a Sclavonian and inherits the title of his Father who is dead. He declares that he has a right to select his wife himself, and though he has never spoken ten words to my daughter or one word out of my presence he requests that he may have the liberty of doing so after I shall be in possession of all the satisfactory renseignments. Until then he will leave Vevay [*sic*] where we have met him in the Salon of the Hôtel or at the dinner table. My daughter is as yet quite ignorant of all these details, and his own scrupulous delicacy upon this point is not the least attractive trait in his character."

Poor Miss Peters! With a dazzled scheming mama and a clever ingratiating Sclavonian Duc, what chance has she! But she was saved, saved by her own good sense. Mrs. Peters writes again to say that the whole thing is off, and shrewd woman that she is, begins the letter with a reference to possible scandal. "Fortunately my daughter had not the least sentiment in his favor. And as she has never seen him except in my presence no *talk* or any disagreeable circumstance can occur. I own I was myself a little influenced by a pleasant exterior and a high sounding title [here we begin to think better of Mrs. Peters] and did not feel that I had a right to refuse my daughter what might have been for her a brilliant fate, but she has promptly and decidedly refused it herself—and even were there no other reasons for her refusal than her indifference to him. [Splendid Miss Peters!] I feel convinced that it is all for the best. It is not enough that he should be duc de Medumn to make her happy." And she ends with a comment on the kindness and good judgment of the Minister which gives us confidence in his dealings with his wandering fellow-citizens.

What did he do about the dentist who put Dayton's name as a reference on his professional card and thus lured Mr. James Rose into entrusting him with a difficult operation in which he was unsuccessful but for which he charged £57 7s. od.? What (in the intervals of combating the French outcry over the "Trent" case) did he do about Mrs. Andrade, who writes "in greatest agony" on pink stationery to say that "nothing but a *personal* visit can give you an idea of what I am subjected to now. My room is locked & I have not even clothes *or my medicine* my husband brutally telling me I could go without *both*. I am here insulted grossly by the concierge who dares to enter where [when] I am *undressed*—above *all* dear Sir, the *precious letters*, on which depends my *all* of defence against the *pitiless* falsehoods and unscrupulous rascalities of M^r. Andrade are in my room, of which he has the keys." The rest of the letter is even more agitated and heart-rending; one sees the liquid eye and hears the throb of the television voice, until one is brought up sharply, as surely Mr. Dayton must have been again and again, by the possibility that it was all true—that husbands do beat their wives, that men of good family (as other correspondence reveals) do continue to cash worthless checks, that mates of ships do mistreat the crew, that young orphans are held in squalor and ignorance away from their proper guardians.

The war at home continues its bloody uncertain way, Motley writes from Vienna that European opinion was never more against the United States, anonymous letters revile the government he is representing, the secessionists gather for a dinner at Philippe's to celebrate a victory against the North, the dispatches pour out daily to Seward, and then, after three years and more in Paris, the accumulations of strains great and small take their toll. Dayton in 1864 was only fifty-seven, but we begin to hear of frequent headaches, that because of an indisposition he missed an appointment with Drouyn de Lhuys, that he did not feel up to accompanying his wife on a trip through Switzerland.

One night in early December of 1864, after dining at home with his family, the United States Minister rode with his son in a cab to the Palais Royal Arcade, where they walked along slowly together conversing and looking into the shop windows, until young William decided to go to the Palais Royal theater nearby. The Minister continued on alone to the Hôtel du Louvre.

It is at this point that mystery enters into the account, for we do not know why Mr. Dayton went to the Hôtel du Louvre; the stories differ, the implications shift. The circumstances and events, even at this distance of time, arouse the liveliest curiosity; one suspects that their unraveling might give one a glimpse of espionage and counter-espionage in the capitals of Europe during the American Civil War. Certainly one would want to know more about Lizzie St. John Eckel, of whom Mr. Dayton had written on January the first of that same year that she was the widow of a late consul of the United States in Chile who "brings to me letters of introduction of the best character. She is a most intelligent cultivated & lady-like person." It was at her apartment in the Hôtel du Louvre that he arrived a little past eight on that December night in the grip of a blinding headache. "Lead me to a seat," he said, "for I can't see." In little more than an hour he was dead, of apoplexy, reported the Minister's doctor.

His son, writing a few days later to an uncle in Camden, says that at the last his father's thoughts turned toward home and the friends he had left there. "Having asked her to play to him some American airs, accompanying herself on her guitar she sang for him, the 'Star Spangled Banner' 'Auld Lang Syne' and 'Home Sweet Home.' He conversing with her all the time, 'Oh!' said he 'Those old airs take me back again to my country among my friends. I wish I were there again practising my profession.'"

The poignancy of that last cry—"I wish I were there again practising my profession"—tells one so much about Dayton's longing for his familiar and accustomed place away from the vexing, trying, troubled responsibilities of the legation, that it touches the heart more nearly than less prosaic words would have done. The splendors of Paris, the glittering variety of Europe, the proud sense of being at the heart of great events give way to a simple, painfully felt longing for the law offices at Trenton, with familiar voices and familiar faces and familiar precedented problems to deal with.

An Error of Judgement and not of the Heart

Amongst the twenty-five thousand or so pieces of the Samuel L. Southard Papers in the Princeton Library[1] there is a handful of letters which delight and tantalize, so much do they tell, so much do they conceal. The historian of politics, of finance, of temperance movements, antislavery, Antimasonry, and other grave and significant affairs in the early nineteenth century would impatiently push aside these red-waxed letters and Mr. Southard's drafts of answers, but to the frivolous observer of human nature they tell a lively little tale of intrigue, vanity, possibly of a broken heart, certainly of a wounded ego or two or three. Indeed they provide the material for a domestic comedy that Trollope could have happily developed, a comedy played against the stately background of Washington but concerned only with very private affairs.

There are three chief characters: Samuel Southard, his daughter Virginia, and one O. Sprigg. Because of the extraordinary chance that preserved these papers and brought them to the Library, we know a great deal about the first two. Southard, a lawyer who was at various times a member of the New Jersey Assembly and governor of the state, a trustee of both the College of New Jersey and the Princeton Theological Seminary, once Secretary of the Navy, and in the period in which we are concerned a United States Senator, was deeply devoted to his family, as the letters he wrote them and especially the letters they wrote to him abundantly demonstrate. Virginia, his only daughter, was an amusing, high-spirited, lightly witty girl who took her father rather less seriously than her two brothers did; she was twenty-one when the first letter

[1] For a brief description of these papers, see "The Samuel L. Southard Papers," *The Princeton University Library Chronicle*, XX, No. 1 (Autumn, 1958), 45-47.

from O. Sprigg was written. Our knowledge of *his* character depends entirely upon these few letters, and so for a clue to his attitudes and actions we must turn to historical records, which are scanty and scattered, but helpful.

His background was excellent. Spriggs had been among the earliest arrivals in Maryland: Thomas Sprigg appears twice on Lord Baltimore's rent rolls, once as Lord of Northampton Manor, Prince George's County, and once as the owner of a property of 137 acres called Bear Garden in Prince George's County which was surveyed for him in 1703.[2] George Washington "Dined at Mr. Sprig's [in Annapolis] and went to the Play in the Evening," September 29, 1773.[3] "O. Sprigg" was one of the signers of the "Proclamation of the Freemen of Maryland" on July 26, 1775,[4] and "Osborne Sprigg," possibly the same man, signed the "Ratification of the Constitution of the United States by the Maryland Convention" in 1788.[5] Over the years the family connections were with the Mercers, the Stocketts and Harwoods of Anne Arundel, the Dorseys and Carrolls of Elk Ridge, and the Bowies of Prince George's County. O. Sprigg's grandfather, the fourth Thomas Sprigg, had married Elizabeth Galloway, who inherited Cedar Park, "probably the oldest large dwelling-house in Maryland," which had been built by her grandfather.[6] O. Sprigg's father was adopted after *his* father's death in 1800 by his uncle Osborn Sprigg, "owner of a large estate in Prince George's county."[7] Though the only Sprigg to be even faintly a national figure[8] was our Sprigg's father, the Hon. Samuel Sprigg, who was governor of Maryland from 1819 to 1822, I think we can safely deduce a background of handsome houses and estates peopled with the aristocracy of Maryland, many of whom were cousins or kissing cousins. We can with even greater safety deduce the confidence that such a background supports and the pride that it fosters.[9]

2 Hester D. Richardson, *Side-Lights on Maryland History*, Baltimore, 1913, I, 266 and 307.

3 *The Diaries of George Washington, 1748-1799*, ed. John C. Fitzpatrick, Boston, 1925, II, 125.

4 Richardson, I, 374.

5 James McSherry, *History of Maryland*, 2nd ed., Baltimore, 1849, p. 400.

6 *The National Cyclopædia of American Biography*, New York, 1893-1958, IX, 300; John M. Hammond, *Colonial Mansions of Maryland and Delaware*, Philadelphia, 1914, pp. 144-[147].

7 Henry F. Powell, comp., *Tercentenary History of Maryland*, Chicago, 1925, IV, 50-51.

8 There is no Sprigg in the *Dictionary of American Biography*.

9 An avenue that tempts exploration is the Princeton connection of the two families. Samuel L. Southard was graduated with the Class of 1804, his two sons with

But of O. Sprigg himself we know very little. He was, one infers, a *young* young man. His health, one gathers, was not good. He had the greatest respect for his father, and he was probably skillful at wheedling or bullying his mother, who, as is so often the case, was more persuadable than his father. He makes his first appearance in a letter to Mr. Southard of October 21, 1836, and his second rather precipitously four days later.

My Dr Sir   Northampton Oct 21st 1836

Owing to circumstances which have heretofore been beyond my control, and during the existence of which I considered any communication to you unnecessary as well as inexpedient, I have delayed to a much later period than I otherwise should have done, mentioning to you a subject upon which I feel sensible you should have been the first consulted.

My attachment to your daughter I am sure you have long been aware of, and as I have reason to beleive the feelings I entertain towards her are favourably received, it only remains necessary for me to request the permission of yrself and Mrs Southard to our engagement. My situation and connexion in life you are so well acquainted with, that I deem any remarks with respect to them superfluous, and will only add that this communication is made with the knowledge and entire approbation of my Parents.

Trusting Sir that my delay in consulting you upon this matter, will be attributed by you entirely to the reasons given above, and not to any want of inclination on my part, and hoping that my wishes may meet with the approbation of yrself and Mrs Southard, I remain yrs

resp^{ly} & truly

Hon^l Saml L Southard   O Sprigg

My Dr Sir   Oct 25th 1836

I wrote you a short letter on Friday last in which I mentioned that but for the existence of certain circumstances, I should have consulted you at a much earlier period about the matter which was the subject of that letter. Circumstances which have since transpired render it necessary on y^r account as well as for my own justification, that I should candidly inform you of the reasons for my long silence. The sentiments of attachment and affection which

---

the Class of 1836. Samuel Sprigg was graduated in 1806, Osborn in 1834. Even if the fathers in their time and the sons in theirs did not know each other, they at least shared a Princeton background with all that that implies.

I entertain for y^r daughter are as you know not of very recent date, from the moment those feelings were first excited, I encouraged and cherished them with the hope and beleif that they would contribute to my future welfare and happiness, and they had taken too firm possession of my breast to be easily eradicated, before I had the least suspicion that I should meet with any difficulty to impede or prevent the consummation of my wishes. Upon consulting my family I met to my astonishment with opposition, but beleiving that opposition arose from causes which would be speedily removed, I thought it the wiser plan to delay broaching the subject to you, untill I could do so with the approbation of my family. When I wrote you on Friday it was under the impression that they were both now disposed to yeild to my wishes, that beleif arose from a conversation I had just had with my mother, whom I found perfectly reconciled to my determination, and I beleived from what she said I should meet with no difficulty with Father who was not then at home. Actuated by a most earnest desire to inform you of my feelings and intentions about this matter and thinking that I was justified from what my mother had told me in beleiving I had the consent of both my Parents I wrote the letter I then did, and I now feel it an indispensable duty owed to you, to tell you frankly that I was deceived, and that I still meet with opposition from my Father, and though it cannot alter or affect my feelings and wishes with regard to your daughter, I could not take the responsibility of concealing the fact from you and allow you to be under an erroneous impression about the matter caused by anything which had fallen from me. Having now Sir told you frankly and candidly all the circumstances connected with the case, and my reasons for never before mentioning the subject to you, I feel desirous of knowing your opinion upon the subject. And in conclusion let me hope Sir that the course I have pursued, will be attributed by you to the real motive and earnest desire to insure the success of my wishes, if you think I have acted unwisely and should have given you this information before, beleive it was an error of judgement and not of the heart. Please direct y^r letter to Washington.

Y^{rs} truly
O Sprigg

Poor O. Sprigg! To have been so bold on the 21st and so humble on the 25th! What *had* Father said when he returned home and was told of his son's proposal? No hint as to the reasons Father had for forbidding the engagement are given, but that the oppo-

34

sition was formidable we can guess by the fact that it looms so large in young Sprigg's mind when he writes the second time as to affect his very phrasing and make him reveal more than he probably wished to. There is more candor than tact in such phrases as "now disposed to *yeild* to my wishes," "perfectly *reconciled* to my determination," "no *difficulty* with Father." It must be admitted, however, that it was a troublesome letter to write and that it was a shrewd stroke on Sprigg's part to leave the decisive action to Mr. Southard.

One would, in fact, sigh more plaintively over his plight if in addition to his fright and confusion he had shown some real feeling in his first letter, some unhappiness in his second. He speaks coolly enough of his "attachment" to Virginia, confidently asserts that his feelings are "favourably received," and with negligent pride refers to his "situation and connexion in life." He has thought about his own "future welfare and happiness," but he doesn't mention Virginia's. One can envisage O. Sprigg, an elegant young man in tight trousers and a handsome waistcoat, cajoling his mother into a statement that he could interpret as consent: O. Sprigg was an only son, and mothers of only sons are very vulnerable to pressure. Fathers are made of sterner stuff. Doubtless O. Sprigg hoped that Father, faced with a *fait accompli*, would give in, but he miscalculated.

How did Virginia feel about this unfortunate withdrawal? We have two glimpses, the first in a note written in a hasty hand and addressed on the back only to "Father," in which she says:

The enclosed came with one for me, & after reading my own, I took the *liberty* of opening your's. Please to answer it, *kindly* for my sake & as soon as you can for it has been several days—let me know how you wish me to act—& then let the subject be no more mentioned. Mother knows nothing of this last, & if possible, I do not wish her to know of its contents.

Will you let me see your answer?   V

Is not this surprising? No stamping of the feet, no flashing eyes, no tears, no plea for pity—just a tender regard for the man who has put her in a humiliating position: "Please to answer it, *kindly* for my sake & as soon as you can for it has been several days."

Mr. Southard's reply[10] was not written until the 31st of October

10 All of Southard's letters here quoted are rough drafts, with many deletions and insertions. I have given them as nearly as I can determine in the form in which they presumably were sent.

and is, it seems to me, a model of tact and generosity. Was O. Sprigg so young that Southard was only amused, was the Hon. Samuel Sprigg so important that Southard was unwilling to be brusque, had Virginia's plea persuaded him to be forbearing? Whatever was in Mr. Southard's mind, he says, with dignity:

Dear Sir:

Your letter of the 21 Oct. reached me as I was leaving home for one of my courts. That of the 25th I found here on my return, last evening. I regret your misapprehension relative to the opinion & wishes of your father, as a correct understanding on that point would have saved you the necessity of writing and me the unpleasant reflection which the subject has occasioned. I do not doubt, however, that you have, in all respects, acted with pure & honorable feelings—and that your error was one of accident, not intention.

I rejoice that the error was corrected before I gave any answer to your first letter. It is unnecessary now, to say what that answer would have been. The fact you mention is conclusive with me & would be so under all circumstances, whatever my feelings & wishes might otherwise dictate. I can never consent that my daughter should go into any family which is not entirely & cheerfully willing to receive her. She could not be happy, with her feelings, in such a condition, & I am too proud of her & love her too well, to permit her to become the wife of any man whom I have ever yet seen, or to enter any family which I have ever yet known where her presence was not desired. My own pride & her acknowledged merit & worth, utterly forbid it.

With this distinct avowal of my opinions & feelings & the expression of personal regard for yourself

I am respl &c

Mr. O. Sprigg   Trenton 31 Oct 1836

Virginia has the last word in this episode of the comedy. In a letter written from Trenton to Mr. Southard in Washington, she says:

Trenton. Monday.

You expressed a wish, my dear Father that I should write to my [sic] my thoughts and feelings on a certain subject—and I have undertaken to comply with your request, though I scarcely know how to speak, or what to say.

Philip Ashton Rollins
By Gutzon Borglum

Keokuk's silver Peace medal with its deerskin pouch

KEE-O-KUCK OR THE WATCHING FOX
The present Chief of the Sauk tribe and Successor to Black Hawk.

Keokuk
James O. Lewis, *The Aboriginal Port-Folio,* Philadelphia, 1835-[36]

Wm L. Dayton.

College of New Jersey
Princeton. Dec. 2. 1862

My dear Sir,

Permit me to introduce to your acquaintance Mr Charles Beaston Jr. of Delaware. Mr Beaston is a graduate of our College, having been admitted to the 1st Degree in the Arts in 1860. He is now in Paris pursuing his studies there. While a Student here, he maintained a good standing as a scholar; and he had the respect of his teachers & of his fellow students.

With the highest respect,
Yours &c
John Maclean

Hon. Wm L. Dayton.

President Maclean introduces a fellow-alumnus

M

Madame William Lewis Dayton, Monsieur Ferdinand Van Der Veer Dayton, Monsieur William Lewis Dayton, Monsieur Edward Lewis Dayton, Mademoiselle Annie Lewis Dayton ont l'honneur de vous faire part de la perte douloureuse qu'ils viennent de faire en la personne de Monsieur *William Lewis Dayton*, Envoyé Extraordinaire & Ministre Plénipotentiaire des États Unis d'Amérique en France, leur époux & père, décédé à Paris, le 1er Décembre 1864, à l'âge de 57 ans.

Imp. Sumy, 8 rue d'Alger, 5 & 10, P.

Announcement of the death of William L. Dayton

ought to close the discussion — this feeling — so far as to exhib. an unbecoming little
ness of ex & at the idea of being foll. by any one
especially by any W & letter Writ ogden & others of
those they & power. men with whom he was
associated. — But my dear & I am tired
of writing & you will be of reading what I
have written & which I ought to furnish you with an example of acc? in writing, yet I am compelled to either to send
this scrawl uncorrected or leave your letter
unanswered for some days — you must
take it as it is — And in consel. I ask you
ask, how do you think P. acq? his powers,
In the same way that you must hereafter
learn to rise hereafter to em. in the prof.
you may choose — to qualify yours. to serve
yours. men & render more than happy
that father & those &c. who watch your progr. with aching anxiety — He had an un-
chart. love of eminence — a perfect devotion
to the acqn of knowl — Labored almost
without ceasing — During the day he studied
while he might — at night he retired early
no matter in what comp? he was — &
found & suff? no just — but hours after mid-
found him at his labors — it is wonderful
that he did not sink sooner under it — and
I do believe that his —

Page 7 of Samuel L. Southard's letter on William Pinkney

From life by Wm H. Brown.

lith. of E.B & E.C Kellogg.

SAMUEL LEWIS SOUTHARD.

Entered according to act of Congress, in the year 1844, by E.B. & E.C Kellogg, in the Clerks Office of the District Court of Connecticut.

The letter written to you by M^r. S— had my entire sanction. I wished most earnestly that it could have been written earlier—for I felt that on such a subject I had no right or desire to use concealment towards such a parent as Heaven has blessed me with. But there was opposition—& I did not choose to let you be spoken to till other parties had yielded their consent. To your decision after the receipt of the second letter I yield—and though I mourn its necessity, I cannot but approve its wisdom. I could & I would not upon any consideration enter a family which did not wish me, even if I stood alone in the world—but *your* daughter shall not be won, unsought. Still, my dear Father, I cannot change my feelings towards S—he has done nothing to offend, or to injure him in my estimation. I believe him to be noble, high-minded & generous—incapable of doing aught mean or ungentlemanly—& while I think so I must feel towards him as I do. I wished you if you met him, to be kind towards him—for my sake do. His health is bad—his physician says excitement is injurious to him—and in his present state, were he to find your manner more cold, it would distress him excessively. I do not believe him consumptive—but if his family persist in their present blind course towards him—wound him as they are now doing, he will die—& that before long. A little advice from you, kindly given, would be welcomed. Kindness will win him sooner than any I ever saw—but his family do not even appear to believe that he can be sick.

I know not his Father's objection—whether it is one that can be removed, or whether it is my poverty or something else equally unalterable. Let it be what it may, till it is removed, we cannot meet—and I fear, if it is not soon done, we shall not meet often in this world. If this is so, I must meet it, and bear it as I can. Though I cannot say, in this state of things, yet I will not confess myself unhappy. It would be ingratitude to Heaven & you, for all the blessings which surround me. I am often a wilful headstrong child—but in my heart I have never faltered in my deep devotion to you. I have struggled & will struggle with myself & my sadness for your sakes. There are *trials* I cannot avert—but as long as I can bear them, I will, and I would suffer ten times more than I do, could I make your home always peaceful & bright. If you answer this, direct your letter to me, and then I can get it—for I do not wish Mother to know aught of this, as long as it can be kept from her.

We are all well—I am going to walk to the office with this—

as the afternoon is pleasant & I feel anxious to feel the fresh air again. . . . Yrs. ever V.

P.S. This is *No. 2* from me let me know whether it reaches you. I fear to trust any thing *private* to the Mails.

It is, I think, an admirable letter; she might be permitted a little hysteria, a little self-pity, but she writes with candor, with affection and concern for her vacillating suitor, and with feeling and respect for her father. She was not a meek acquiescent model of filial decorum, but a spirited young person, as the many letters from her to her father and brothers amply demonstrate, and the self-control and maturity displayed here are therefore all the more striking.

Some fifteen months later, young Sprigg, now coming out from behind the round O to sign himself Osborn, writes again, and, granted that the opening is not auspicious in a lover and that he is naturally nervous, even though he now has Father's consent in making his second overture, he does appear to be moved by feeling as well as by agitation.

Dear Sir   Washington Jan 24th 1838
It becomes my duty once more to address you upon a subject, which it was my lot once before to do under circumstances peculiarly distressing to me. I have again Sir to express a hope that the renewal of the connexion formerly existing between a member of your family and myself may not be unpleasant to you, I have reason to beleive that the feelings of yr daughter remain unchanged and have to give you the assurance that mine have done so from the moment they were first expressed. I have consulted my Parents upon the subject again and make this communication not only with their knowledge and consent but with their expressed desire that it should be done. My Father will communicate with you upon the subject verbally or by letter in the course of a few days. In the mean time my Dr Sir I trust I am not too sanguine in cherishing the confident hope, that you will not allow the reminiscence of unpleasant circumstances, arising from misapprehension, to influence yr decision upon a question of such deep interest to all parties concerned. Trusting that my wishes herein expressed may meet with the approbation of yrself and Mrs Southard
                    I remain very resply yrs
                                   Osborn Sprigg

He waits three days and has no reply. He writes again.

Dr Sir   Washington Saturday
Not having yet received as I hoped I should have done, an
acknowledgement of the receipt of a communication made you
on Wednesday last, induces me to make enquiry of it's safe de-
livery, and to request that it may meet with the earliest attention
y^r convenience will permit, being a subject of anxiety to me.
                              Very resptly Y^r ob^t sr^{vt}
                              Osborn Sprigg

Mr. Southard's cool and stern rebuke in answer must have
stung. He says:

O. S. Esq,
Dear Sir,
Your note of last evening has been rec^d. Your letter of Wednesday last was not seen by me, until Thursday morning, as I was
leaving my lodgings to make an argument in the Supreme Court.
My engagements, since that, in the Senate & the Court, have been
incessant, & would have prevented my writing to you before this
time, even if I had supposed it necessary or expedient to write, in
great haste, under all the circumstances which have transpired.
You recollect that as long ago as October 1836 you wrote me
a letter on the same subject under misapprehension of the wishes
of your parents, & that, before I had an opportunity to acknowledge it, I rec^d. another informing me of their decided opposition
to your wishes. The feelings which I entertained, at that time,
were communicated to you, and I refer you to my letter, for sentiments which I assure you are, in no degree changed.
Since it was written, now 15 months ago, I had heard nothing
on the subject, until yours of Wed^y. last came to me. It created
as you may suppose some surprise. As you again informed me
that your parents were willing that you should make a communication to me—as you add—"My father will communicate with
you on the subject verbally or by letter, in the course of a few
days"—and as, in the mean time, you did not request an answer,
I did not suppose, until your note of yesterday, that you would
expect one quite so promptly, or that any feeling of courtesy or
respect could demand it quite so hastily.
The circumstances which had already occurred had been suffi-
ciently painful—& I was not willing even to consult the wishes of

my daughter, until I was, myself, in a better condition to judge & to advise her. I cannot consent that she shall be harassed by appeals to her feelings, which may, by *possibility*, lead only to their being wounded. The state of your health ought, with all parties, to have influence & there are matters to which it is not necessary to allude, but which may affect the decision. And I have had less solicitude for an early explanation with her, because, what ever may be her inclinations, I know, she has sufficient firmness & pride of character to yield to nothing which may not comport entirely with her judgement & her sensibility to her own honor & that of her parents.

I am respectfully &c

What, pray, are these "matters to which it is not necessary to allude"? That Southard might be willing to bedevil Osborn and his father a little by delay, one can sympathetically believe; indeed what is teasing is the fact that he obviously wants to delay a definite reply until he has had the interview with the Hon. Samuel Sprigg, who seems less than eager for the encounter. Were the "matters to which it is not necessary to allude" to be made clear then? Did Southard anticipate the sweet savor of apology and petition, or the sharp satisfaction of attack?

His letter provided no balm to young Sprigg, who now began to be alarmed. The letter that follows is a stiff-necked one, asking the same question that we do and reflecting more his offended dignity than any intention to supplicate a favorable reply.

Hon^l Saml L Southard   Washington Monday
Dr Sir

I regret that the note I addressed you evening before last should have been looked upon by you as importunate, and hope that the request it contained will not be attributed to any discourteous or disrespectful feeling, but simply to the deep agitating anxiety natural to a subject so important. I should now after having heard from you remain passive and await y^r leisure and inclination for a satisfactory reply. But a portion of the contents of that letter alters the complexion of the case, and obliges me in justice to myself once more to apply to you for information. When enabled to remove the *only objection* ever stated to me, I had hoped that much time would not be required to make me happy in your approbation, but fear from the paragraph in your letter that "there are other circumstances not now necessary to allude to which may influence your decision" objections are now entertained of which

I am ignorant. To discover what these may be is the object I now have in addressing you, I shall be willing and most happy at any time to meet any examination or scrutiny into my conduct, originating from one whose right to enquire into it *I* acknowledge. I appeal therefore most respectfully to your honour and generosity to acquaint me with them, as soon as your kind [?] leisure will permit.

Very resptly Y^r obt srvt

Osborn Sprigg

We now have a letter which properly speaking does not belong in the Southard Papers, since it was not written by or to him. How it got into Mr. Southard's hands we can only guess; that it did so we can be gleefully grateful, for it introduces an important minor character and gives us a glimpse into the machinery of the comedy.

The letter is from Osborn, and, though it begins "My Dr Grand mother," is addressed to Miss M. G. Meade. Now a later very interesting letter to Virginia which is signed "Margaret" indicates that Virginia had been calling Margaret "Nannie," and one gathers that under this playful name Miss Meade had been acting as an aider and abettor, a go-between, a romantic sympathizer and confidante of both parties. She was evidently a girl who liked variety in nomenclature, for in her earlier appearances in the Southard Papers she signs herself "Jack" and "Mag" and "M." (Fortunately Southard in his careful way wrote her name on the back of the letters.) Though brief, they are full of bounce and banter: "If you have a letter for me from Trenton for the love of mercy send it down to me. I have not heard from Virginia for a week, and (between you and I) I am most *terribly unhappy.*" "I trust that you arrived in good health and as soon as you have nothing better to do that you will allow me to give you just such a greeting as I did last year."

Certainly when Osborn writes to Margaret he is completely at ease; he expects her to have information and to give it to him freely; his letter implies a little nexus of conspiracy and complicity including even a shadowy Cousin Sally. There is candor in Osborn's letter, a candor which, it is noticeable, reveals a certain bridling and restlessness, but even to a confidante no sighs, no passion. He does not propose any rash action; *if* Virginia, he says, "will convince me that it [is] her desire and intention to persevere," he will take steps! Osborn even in his unguarded mo-

41

ments does not sound like a young man overwhelmed and blind with love.

The letter is undated but clearly is concerned with the events of January, 1838. It is signed only with an initial S, but it is written in Osborn's unmistakable slanted hand and with the fine-pointed pen that he always used. "My Dr Grand mother," it begins:

You asked me this morning if I would be at home by seven o'clock presuming you had some particular motive for enquiring I herewith report myself as at my post. From y^r note to Cousin Sally I suppose you expect a note from V, has it arrived and if so does it contain anything by which I could procure a hint of the existing state of affairs in her household. I am totally at a loss what to do, the continued silence with which my letter has been treated is most unaccountable to me if it is not noticed within the next two days, I shall have but one of two courses to adopt either to abandon the affair or to make application in *person* for an answer, and I shall be regulated in my choice by the opinion of Virginia expressed to me if I can elicit one from her. If upon application to her she will convince me that it [is] her desire and intention to persevere, I will make a personal demand for an answer of some sort, as he seems determined not to notice a written communication. There was company here this morning when my Father was about starting which prevented his writing, he stopped at the Capitol however to write M^r S a note which will be delivered in an envelope to me by Mr Carroll this evening when he gets home. But that note I cannot send to M^r S untill he chooses to answer my letter or I have an interview with him. To do so would betray a want of self respect on my part, and a want of justice to my Father, who was as kind as Parent could be upon the subject and perfectly willing to do anything I might require of him. He came up for no other purpose than because he thought I would wish him to go to see M^r S, but as matters now stand I could not ask him to do it, I would not have allowed him to go there as *mediator* for me even if he would have done so, if M^r S had any objections to urge *I* am the person to look to for an explanation. Did you see V today and how was she.   Y^{rs} truly
                                                                        S

Meanwhile one may be sure that whatever affairs of state might occupy the senator from New Jersey, the proposal and its implications and reverberations were much thought on. With relish, perhaps? With regrets that Virginia was beyond the spanking stage? At any rate, in an admirable display of restraint, tact, and dignity he finally writes to Osborn Sprigg and his father.

O. Sprigg Esq
Dear Sir,

Since I had an interview with your father two days ago, I have reflected anxiously on the subject of your last note to me—& conversed with those most deeply interested in the matter. And it is now, my duty to say—that it is our united wish that the subject should not be any further prosecuted. In coming to this decision, I beg you to believe, that it is done in no unkind nor unfriendly temper, but we have all been influenced by considerations which belong to such an occasion. Having heretofore enjoyed a friendly intercourse with you & your family, we are unwilling that what we have resolved, should be attributed to any feeling which would demand its discontinuance.

I think it proper to write a letter to your father which I shall do tomorrow.

Dear Sir,

After my interview with you two days ago at the Capitol, I took the first occasion to converse with my wife & daughter. The result of our united reflections have led to a letter of which I think it proper to enclose you a Copy. In doing so, I hope you will believe that the answer has been given, with a full sense of its importance, & with the most respectful feelings toward you Mrs S. & your son. I beg also to add, that your language manner & feelings on this occasion, have added another to the many evidences which I have had of your frank & honorable character.

I am sincerely & respectfully &c &c

Saml L. Southard

Hon Saml. Sprigg   Wash^n. 7 Feb. 1838

Osborn Sprigg clearly did not enjoy receiving his letter from Mr. Southard. In the two weeks that had elapsed between his second proposal and Mr. Southard's reply to it, he had had plenty of time for interpretation of the silence and for contemplation of the outcome, but he was not prepared for a refusal. He writes for an explanation—it is his due, one feels, for Mr. Southard certainly gave no reason for the refusal either to the Hon. Samuel

Sprigg or to Osborn. Within the week after Southard's letters were drafted, Osborn writes to him:

Hon[l] Sam[l] L Southard   Washington Febry 13th 1838
D[r] Sir

Y[r] letter of the 7th inst was duly received, and it is hardly necessary for me to assure you of my sad disappointment at it's contents. It should have been answered immediately upon it's receipt, but not having seen my Father since his interview with you, I was desirous of first acquainting myself with the tenor of that conversation before answering your note. Since I have done so I must acknowledge that y[r] letter has not only disappointed but surprised me. In the first letter you wrote me, you refer me to y[r] letter of 1836 for sentiments which you say "have in no degree changed" & reperusal of that letter only confirms the impression first made upon me when it was received, viz. that there was but the one objection entertained by yrself, such I have been led to beleive was the case from the first agitation of this matter, after a conversation with my Father with which you express your entire satisfaction, it was not presumptive in me to hope for a favorable reception of my application. That having been denied me I am irresistibly led to the conclusion, that there are circumstances the existence of which I am not aware of, which have influenced y[r] decision. It is to request you to assign some reason for this change in y[r] sentiments that I have written this. I assured you in a former letter of my willingness to meet any objections you might have to urge, do not then I pray you Sir treat my feelings with so little consideration as to thus laconically dismiss a subject in which my happiness is involved. I am sure Sir that upon consideration you will acknowledge the justice of this request and not refuse it.

Very resptly yrs
Osborn Sprigg

And as for Margaret, the confidante, she is thrown into a frenzy by the news. The letter from her to Virginia has been penciled on two scraps of paper that have been folded very small; one imagines that the billet was slipped surreptitiously into Virginia's hand. Its presence among the Southard Papers and that of Osborn's to her hint that Virginia had had to make a clean breast of the whole tissue of intrigue and had turned over to her father these interesting documents. Margaret's is particularly affecting. It begins breathlessly without address:

I have hardly time dear Virginia to answer your note just received I will endeavor to do so some time to day altho I think the less said upon the subject the better I have but *one* regret as regards the affair between ourselves and that is that I should have said any thing against your Father, for this I trust I may be forgiven As regards *yourself* I am still too sensitive the change in your ideas and feelings are *too sudden* for me to venture upon the subject. My peculiar disposition has been too often discussed for me to repeat that I must be blind to the defects of those I love to idolize them as I have done you, however you shall never see the change in my feelings if I can help it and I will *try* to love as when I thought you perfection it is not that you have discarded S but it is the inconsistency of your course and your conduct with another, when his fate was in your hands that has almost broken my heart. The only consolation left me now is to soothe and bring his mind and feelings to their proper state and in this I trust God will take mercy on him and give me the power of effecting it. I shall go over with your note in my hand and a melancholly scene I shall go through and then *all* will be over. I would come down and see you today, but I would rather defer it until I am myself again. When that will be heaven only knows I shall however be glad to see you whenever you feel inclined to come but you must not call me Nannie that name is connected with happier hours and if I am to *forget* I must have nothing to remind me of the past. Oh Virginia why have you deceived me so and told me what you did not feel you have made me do that for which I *never* can forgive myself but come to me as soon as you can let me have one talk with you and then I will do as I have promised Dont be angry with me for speaking plainly I cannot deceive you and make believe that I see no fault ever your friend Margaret

Margaret's impulsive nature, which has led her rashly to criticize Mr. Southard, which charges Virginia with deceit and inconsistency, supplies more emotion than the lover ever has done. One is glad that, after all her accusations, she still signs herself "ever your friend."

Mr. Southard's reply to Osborn was this time more difficult to write. It is carefully composed, with many deletions and insertions, and the result is firm, detailed, and final; the lawyer's skill is evident in its marshaling of facts, the statesman's in its eloquence.

I have, at length, a few moments to devote to your letter of the 13th which was in answer to mine of the 7th. If my engagements had permitted you should have recd. this at an earlier hour.

It has become painful to me & I am sure must be so to you to continue our correspondence. Constructions & explanations of letters can *now*, be of no real service to either of us.

There are, however one or two matters in your last letter which require a few words from me. You say—"Since I have done so" (that is, acquainted yourself with the conversation between your father & myself) "I must acknowledge that your letter" (of the 7th) "has not only disappointed but surprised me. In the first letter you wrote me, you refer me to your letter of 1836 for sentiments which you say, "have in no degree changed." A reference of that letter only confirms the impression first made upon me when it was recd Viz. that there was but the one objection entertained by yourself. Such I have been led to believe was the case from the first agitation of this matter. After a conversation with my father, with which you express your entire satisfaction, it was not presumption in me to hope for a favorable reception of my application."

I do not doubt that your father has communicated to you the precise substance of our conversation. It manifested on his part, a kind & respectful feeling for me & my family which was entirely reciprocated, on my part, for him & his—& which I have felt, with great sincerity for many years—& see no cause now to change. It exhibited also in him, a deep & proper parental feeling for the happiness of his son—in which I felt a becoming participation. But that conversation also left me, at full liberty, to consider the proposition which you had made, to consult my family & to decide upon it, as my heart & judgment should dictate. And I assure you that that conversation presented the first occasion on which I felt either the power or the inclination, deliberately to consult the matter as one more deeply affecting my own happiness & that of my family, than any which has occurred at any time. Up to that moment I was not at liberty to decide & did not choose to speculate about it.

You refer to my letter of 1836. I regret that I cannot *here* examine it. The construction which you put upon it gives me pain in more aspects than one. If I have expressed the idea that I had but one objection—the opposition of your parents—I have been more incautious than I am wont to be. I meant to say, no such thing. I meant to express *no opinion* or *feeling* in regard to the subject of your first letter. Your second, precluded the *consideration* of that *subject*. It informed me that your parents were opposed to the Union you proposed. That was eno' for me. I certainly did not intend to tell you that I was willing that my daughter should marry you when you told me your parents were opposed to it & thus have left her & my feelings & honor in your & their hands to be dealt with as you might find suited to your inclinations. It was at least proper that I should be assured that your suit would be prosecuted before I offered her to you. I hope I conveyed in my letter no other feeling. I could quite as soon have followed her to her grave as have done this—or permitted her to enter as the wife of an only son a family which had rejected her. And this I say & felt, without the slightest sensation of offence towards your parents. It was a matter for them to decide. It was for you to follow their dictates if you thought them just & right—& I certainly inferred from your silence for so many months that you intended obedience to them. When I wrote my letter therefore I had no sentiment of unkindness or resentment towards you or them. I considered it an occasion on which you had fallen into error as to their wishes—an error by no means culpable—and I tho't you acted with correct & honorable promptitude in apprising me of that error. I had been from home & your second letter was, (I think) recd & read by me on the same day with your first—and I regarded it as putting an end to all necessity on my part, to consider & decide the matter. The whole subject was to me, as if it had not been presented. In this feeling I ans^d. & subsequently regarded it. But surely with that second letter before me, I did not intend to tell you that I had but one objection—the opposition of your parents. This would have been a strange declaration for a father with a letter before him from a young man declaring that he could not marry his daughter. It would have [placed] her & me in the humiliating position of seeking a connexion which was refused. I neither meant to say that I had or I had not objections & I hope my letter of 1836 bears no other construction. All that I ought to have said was that your second letter relieved me from the necessity of making up an opinion about it.

You tell me that I say "my sentiments have in no degree changed." This is strictly true. I probably told you, that I regarded your conduct as honorable—& perhaps felt gratified that you had discovered merits in my child which attracted your affections. This is still so. I may have said that you had acted fairly, in apprising me, at the first moment that you were not permitted to follow your own inclinations. This is also true. I should have suffered much if I had found & announced a willingness to see the union effected, & had afterwards been told that my child had been rejected, by any one on earth. I thought you acted honorably—& I may have told you so. But I did not mean to say that I was willing to have V. marry *any* man, before I knew that that man & his family were willing to receive her. I should as soon think of asking some one whom I met to take her. I supposed I left the whole matter, as if nothing had been said or done in regard to it.

I may have expressed regard for you. I felt it—I feel it now. I believe your conduct has been, thus far, in life—strictly respectable & worthy—& I will not permit any circumstance, not affecting your honor & conduct—to change my opinion, or *induce me to say or do anything inconsistent with my regard for you & your family.* But you must be aware that a thousand considerations intervene when a parent is compelled to decide a question on which the happiness of an *only* & *most beloved daughter* absolutely & irretrievably depend. The health—the profession—the habits of business—the present means of support—the residence—and a multitude of other facts—all present themselves—& have an influence—and yet none of them necessarily affect the honor or integrity of the man who asks to take her from a parents' guardianship & protection.

You demand a reason. Am I bound to give one? The decision is the *united determination* of myself & family, embracing the one most deeply interested, & for whose happiness I have *no earthly* honor or object which I would not sacrifice, without a murmur. Receive it then—& believe that while it is given, there is but one feeling or wish for your prosperity & happiness, in any one of us —& let us close this most painful correspondence.

I am sincerely & respectfully &c &c &c

And then there is added on different paper a note whose stern tone shows that the training of the lawyer and the statesman was not proof against the provocation of an angry young man.

Friday Evening

P.S. Since I wrote this letter V. has put into my hands a note which she has rec^d. from you, of yesterdays date. *Such* a note— ought not to have been written by *you*—to her. The harshness of temper which it displays & the *unjust* imputations which it conveys can receive no answer either from her or from me.

48

She informs me that she has thro' Miss Meade requested you to return some letters of hers. I have, now, for her, to repeat the request.

The note which Mr. Southard so strongly condemns follows:

Thursday

The request made by you of Miss Margaret yesterday, only confirms the fear I had before entertained, that it was not y^r intention now or at any future day to use y^r influence with y^r Father to have his decision with regard to myself revoked. This therefore will I presume be the last note I shall ever have the privilege of writing to you. And now in parting with you Virginia, allow me to give you a peice of advice, prompted by the purest motives, never hereafter to trifle with the feelings of one whose affections you have enthralled, be assured that though for the time being your vanity may be flattered and y^r pride gratified, it cannot eventually add to y^r self respect, and will moreover destroy that greatest of all blessings, a consciousness of having done what y^r best judgement prompted you to.

Treated as I have been without the slightest consideration for my feelings and situation, I am yet willing to confess the deep interest I feel in you, and to acknowledge that I would gladly cling to the most remote hope, were I allowed to beleive that you had not lost all interest in me. That you may succeed in all the *veiws* and *plans* you have formed for the future, and that their accomplishment may insure y^r happiness is my most ardent wish. And if the assurance that you have blighted the hopes of one, whose prospects for the future, were brighter than most persons will add to y^r happiness, it may be a gratification to you to know that you have succeeded. The pain and agony you have caused one, whose very soul was wrapted in *you*, may serve to *amuse* y^r idle moments at some future day.

Farewell—S

Poor O. Sprigg—it is so hard to take him seriously! Whether a constant lover or a revived lover, he does not ever stand up like a man, but must be bolstered, like Sir Andrew Aguecheek, in his proposal, and when he fails his reproaches are plaintive or shrill, not tragic.

But one must nevertheless feel sorry for him at the end: he had without doubt been treated badly. Naughty Virginia, recovered

49

from her first tenderness, innocently assisted by the romantic Margaret and with who knows what wicked memories of the episode of 1836, had quite evidently encouraged him, led him on, wrought him up to making another proposal, one which this time *her* father should refuse. Whether her conscience reproached her for trifling "with the feelings of one whose affections [she had] enthralled," or whether her flattered vanity and gratified pride made the episode one "to *amuse* [her] idle moments," we cannot even guess. The chapter for us is ended with the following announcement, which appeared nine months later in a Baltimore paper, in the column headed "Married":

> At New York, on Thursday evening, by the Rev. Dr. Wainwright, OGDEN HOFFMAN, to VIRGINIA E. SOUTHARD, daughter of the Hon. Samuel L. Southard.

William Pinkney, 1764-1822

The Death of the Man in the Doeskin Gloves

The presentation to the Princeton University Library of a collection of papers of William Pinkney, the gift of Mrs. T. P. Dixon, Jr., enhanced the interest of a document relating to Pinkney found in the papers of Samuel L. Southard which throws new light on Pinkney's contemporary reputation. The enrichment of one collection by materials in another is an always satisfactory and desirable aspect of library acquisitions, an illustration of which principle is amply provided in the document here published.

WILLIAM PINKNEY was a man who excited and exacerbated his contemporaries—his fellow lawyers were alternately irritated by his flamboyance and overwhelmed by his brilliance, and crowds flocked to the visitors' galleries at the Supreme Court when it was known that he was going to speak. Justice Joseph Story, writing to his brother-in-law in March, 1819, says: "We have had a crowded audience of ladies and gentlemen; [when Pinkney spoke] the hall was full almost to suffocation, and many went away for want of room."[1] And this for a two-day speech in the case of Maryland *vs.* the Bank of the United States!

The man who so enthralled and titillated the belles and beaux of Washington was, however, no mere orator. Though "a man who, at the age of fifty, spoke in amber-colored doeskin gloves, could hardly be expected to have a taste for simple and natural elocution,"[2] his industry was as passionate as his rhetoric, and forced his opponents to like exertions. Attorney General William Wirt called him "that 'damned magician Glendower,' " and said that "a debate with Pinkney is exercise and health." On Pinkney's sudden death at the age of fifty-eight, Wirt wrote to a friend, "He is a real loss to the Bar. No man dared to grapple with him without the most perfect preparation, and the full possession of all his

[1] Hampton L. Carson, comp., *Pen Sketches of William Pinkney as he Appeared to his Contemporaries*, reprinted from *The Legal Intelligencer* of February 8, 1895 [n.p., n.d.], pp. 13-14.

[2] *Ibid.*, p. 24.

strength. Thus, he kept the Bar on the alert, and every horse with his traces tight."[3]

Pinkney's death was a matter of some moment to the young American republic, and was widely commented upon. One of the most interesting of the impromptu obituaries of the man was written by Samuel Lewis Southard, whose voluminous papers are now in the possession of the Princeton University Library.[4] In 1822 Southard was serving his second year in the United States Senate. He was then thirty-five and at a moment in his life when the future loomed large and full of promise. His temperament was judicious, serious, and sober; his pious New Jersey background and Presbyterian schooling did not encourage an appreciation of the flamboyant or the unconventional. Because of their contrasting personalities, it is particularly interesting to learn what Southard thought of the legal luminary, brilliant both in plumage and in eloquence, who obviously fascinated him.

Among Southard's papers was found a rough draft of a letter to an unknown person ("Frank"), written at the time of Pinkney's death and describing his personality and accomplishments. Despite Southard's protestations to his correspondent that he is sending merely his unstudied thoughts, the composition of this eight-page letter clearly cost him much study and reflection, as the deletions, broken sentences, and marginal additions on the reproduced page amply demonstrate. They also present considerable difficulty in transcription. Since an exact transcript would be cumbersome and unintelligible, I have attempted to make a smooth-running account, using the phrases that Southard would himself have copied. The insertions are incorporated into the text without comment, the patchy punctuation is systematically supplemented, the abbreviations are expanded, with the letters added in square brackets. The expansion of abbreviations, however, has occasionally had to be the result of divination; such amplified words should be taken as suggestions rather than as certainties. The deletions, which witness Southard's struggle for a clear and telling statement, are italicized within angle brackets. Since Southard did not as a rule indicate where he intended his marginal additions to go in the text, and since it is not always clear just where they would fit in, I have put them all together at the end of the transcript.

3 *Ibid.*, p. 20.

4 See Alexander P. Clark, "The Samuel L. Southard Papers," *The Princeton University Library Chronicle*, XX, No. 1 (Autumn, 1958), 45-47.

My dear Sir,

I was ⟨very⟩ much pleased to see my gold edged paper return, bringing with it, proofs of your good will. ⟨As it has induced you to have gratified gratify me with one letter, I shall trust to your willingness. We have to day a very mel[ancholy] duty to perform to⟩ The edge is not now the most val[uable] part ⟨about⟩ of it. I have just returned from the performance of a mel[ancholy] duty ⟨aiding to restore⟩ restoring to its kind[red] dust ⟨the⟩ all that rem[ained] with us *here* of ⟨W^m⟩ P— ⟨once one⟩ (ten days since, full of life & vigor & hope—now he is senseless alike to the graspings of amb[i- tion] & the resp[ect] of friends—) You will see in the Intell[igencer] of ⟨to day⟩ this morning the marks of respect paid to his memory by Cong[ress] & the Sup[reme] Court. ⟨*His mind was perfectly gigantic*[?]⟩

The scene of to day has been most solemn & impressive. A[t] 10 ⟨*The process*[ion] *left his lodgings & bore to*⟩ his remains were car- ried from his lodgings to the Sen[ate] Ch[amber] where but ⟨a few⟩ 12 days ago, & for the last time, his voice was raised to sustain a claim vs the Gov[ernment] of ⟨the⟩ a widow & her orphan Children. He was then ⟨being⟩ in the full ⟨vigor⟩ exercise of his corporeal & mental powers & able alike to convince the under[standing] & gratify the taste & warm the heart—elevated in reputation & ear- nestly looking forward to still higher elevation. He was now restored to that chamber, senseless alike to the grasping of ambition, the admiration of friends—the respect of the hundreds who sur- rounded him. He was placed directly in front of the Pres[idential] chair, his head towards it. The Ch[airman] of the Sen[ate] was in the Clh.^s [i.e., Chairman's] seat & near him the Phys[ician] who attended thro' the illness. ⟨*On the left of the P*[resident] *was the Sp*[eaker] *of the H*[ouse] *of R*[epresentatives]⟩ On the left of the Coffin ⟨*each in the hab*[its] *of mourning*⟩ were the Sen[ators] & Rep[resentatives] from Mar[yland] & the rel[atives] of the De- c[eased]—on the right, the Com[mittee] of Ar[rangements] & Pall B[earers] ⟨each⟩ all in the habil[iments] of mourning. [Three words deleted.] Behind the Com[mittee] & Pall B[earers] were the Sen- [ators]. Imm[ediately] on the right of the P[resident's] chair were the Judges of Sup[reme] C[ourt] & memb[ers] of the Bar—on the left ⟨*of the Ch*[air]⟩ the 4 Sec[retaries] of the Dep[artments]—two of the for[eign] min[isters] & their suites.

After a pause of some min[utes] the Sp[eaker] with the of[ficers] & mem[bers] of the H[ouse] appeared at the door, the Senate with

53

those who were al⟨l⟩ ready in the room rose to receive them & remained stand[ing] until the Sp[eaker] had taken his place on the left of the Pres[ident] of the Sen[ate] & the Members those which [were] prepared for them on the left of the ⟨Ch[airman]⟩ Pres[ident] & opposite to the ⟨members⟩ Senators. The rest of the ⟨House⟩ room was crouded in every part. A pause of some minutes succeeded—& he who did not then feel ⟨how short⟩ ⟨imp[ressed] at that mom[ent] with the shortness of⟩ how weak is man & how uncertain his hopes must ⟨be⟩ have feelings strangely disorganized. The Ch[airman] rose & in ⟨a⟩ slow & solemn ⟨manner⟩ accents read the 14 Chap[ter] of Job [The next few lines are much crossed out and interlined.] & then closing the book with trembling hand & quiv[ering] lip & with his eye ⟨& hand⟩ directed towards the object before him, begun his address with these words: *again* has this chamber become the place of mourning—*again* [Word deleted.] are we compelled to wit[ness] the frailty of our nature & the

His address was short ⟨&⟩ but impressive—not however to what I have heard him on other occasions. After his address he offered up a short prayer. ⟨*When the process[ion]*⟩ after which the body was carried out & the funeral moved ⟨*in the order detailed in the enclosed paper.*⟩ The number of carriages could not have been less than between two & three hundred, extending the greater part of a mile. ⟨*He was buried*⟩ ⟨*The burying ground is on the Eastern Branch about 1¼ miles from the capitol—and there*⟩ When the process[ion] came near the ⟨*grave*⟩ burying ground which is near the E[astern] B[ranch] about 1¼ mile from the Capitol, it halted & the body was followed to the grave in the order the order [*sic*] detailed in the enclosed paper. When the body was deposited, a short prayer & benediction was pronounced & the process[ion] returned to the Capitol.

Thus ⟨*was closed in the termination*⟩ ended the closing scenes of a splendid life—thus my dear Frank, emphat[ically] passes away the glory of this passing world. ⟨*The man whom we left to moulder in the damp & black valley, was*⟩ He whom we left behind us has been an extraord[inary] man—gifted with powers vastly superior to the great mass of his fell[ow] mort[als] and could I offer him to you as an object altogether worthy of your imitation I would endeavor to draw a portrait of him. In place of this I enclose you a short & not well executed account of him from one of the public prints. It is probably faithful in its detail of facts. In his person he was about 5.9 rather ⟨*fat*⟩ inclined to fatness & ⟨*corpulent*⟩

corpulency but active. Saturnine complexion—round face—⟨with⟩ lips inclined to thickness & rendered more so by a habit of extending them when [sic] both when reading & when engaged in conversation & speaking—a brow somewhat heavy—with no prominence of features, nor any strongly marked outline which we should at once fasten upon as indicative of high daring genius. ⟨his complexion was saturnine & I do no⟩ Had you seen him ⟨without be⟩ as a stranger you would not have selected him ⟨for⟩ as a great man.

In his dress, he appr[oached] to fop[pishness] & dandyism & always had the app[earance] of wearing, tho' I do not believe—He must have spent much time at his toilet—& seemed hard to please in his dress & expensive. It is said that for many years of his life he expended nearly $2000 per year upon his person.

Of his moral character I know little, of his relig[ious] op[inions] I ⟨can⟩ know nothing. The Clergyman in his funeral address declared it as a fact [Nine words deleted.] that he was seriously impress[ed] in the lat[ter] part of his life, with the truth & import[ance] of the Crist[ian] [sic] religion—that he had often seen his eyes ⟨fill⟩ moistened with tears while listening to its doct[rine]— & that a few days before his illness in the Sen[ate] Ch[amber] he had regretted to him the influe[nce] of this world in drawing off its a consideration of the next.

In his pol[itical] opin[ions] & cond[uct] he was not that decided & undev[iating] pol[itician] upon whom reliance is to be had at every moment. And it arose, in a great degree, from his not having paid that steady & uniform attention to the subj[ect] which he always did to his prof[ession]. For whenever he was called upon by his count[ry] to serve her abroad, or his inter[est] or duty req[uired] his attent[ion] to any subject at home, no man was more sure to come to a right conclusion & no man more ably defended that Conclusion.

In his profess[ion] he was prob[ably] the first in his day. He was always devoted to it, in every situation. While coun[sel] in the first inst[ance] ⟨in Lond[on]⟩ & afterwards Emb[assador] in Lond[on] his [sic] was a most labor[ious] stud[ent] & a daily attendant, at [Word deleted.] the Court where Sir Wᵐ Scott presided. It was in this way that he added to his early acquirements & was enabled to lead the bar, & even to instruct the C[ourt] when com[mercial] & adm[iralty] law became so important. In ⟨arg[ument] he was always powerful⟩ the learning of the books he was always ready—in arg[ument] always powerful & irresistible. ⟨*Tho*⟩ sometimes he devoted time & labor & argument ⟨*upon*⟩ to positions not very necess[ary] to the result at which he aimed, & like a giant with a pigmy, trifled with a display of un[necessary?] learning. Such seemed to me the last arg[ument] which he delivered—tho' it is not imp[ossible] that I judge inaccurately in this as I heard but a part of that arg[ument] & was not acq[uainted] with the merits of his cause.

His powers of illustration were unusually good. He made nature & science subservient to the elucidation of his ideas. He was perfectly fam[iliar] with class[ical] writers & constantly rendered them tributary to his wishes. He was enabled to do this by an act of no ordi[nary] self control & effort of ambit[ion]. When he went to L[ondon] as Cons[ul] as is mentioned in the enclosed sketch of his life, he found that his class[ical] learning was unequal to that of his Brit[ish] asso[ciates] among whom at that time a ⟨*kind of*⟩ mad[ness] for that kind of learn[ing] existed—he immediately put himself as a sch[olar] to one of the best teachers in L[ondon] reviewed & extended his class[ical] reading ⟨*learning*⟩ & enjoyed ⟨*always*⟩ to his death the rich benefits of his labor. He was extremely nice & even fas[tidious] in the use both of his own & the dead lang[uages] and sometimes exhibited an almost ludicrous disgust at the want of taste & accuracy in others.

His habits were oppu[lent]—his squand[ering] of money prover[bial]. His salary is said never ⟨*suff.*⟩ to have suf[ficed] him in Eng[land] & when he went to Russ[ia] his two out. [?] & his sal[ary] in all $27,[ooo] did not sustain him. And altho' his practice was imm[ensely] prof[itable] & his fam[ily] econom[ical], yet he laid by for their time of need not more than 30,[ooo] or 40,[ooo] a sum suff[icient] for a caut[ious] econ[omy] but small for a fam[ily] of 10 or 11 Ch[ildren] who have been r'd [reared or raised?] luxuriously.

His man[ner] especially on great occasions was not pleasant to me. ⟨*it smack[ed] of affec[tation] & more of stage effect*⟩ It was not nat[ural] to him nor such as he had before he went to England. It is said that [he] formed it after the celeb[rated] act[or] Kemb[le] in Eng[land] & I think it very prob[able]—⟨*It was not natural to him*⟩ it had in it much of aff[ectation] & more of stage effect. He ⟨*was*⟩ elevated & depressed his voice ext[remely] even in the same sentence—tho' the dep[ression] was not such as to be indist[inct] nor the elev[ation] so great as to be inart[iculate]. His gest[ure] was usually perf[ormed] in the style of Sh[akespearean] actors. When excited he was very vehement & for minutes would press forward in tone man[ner] gest[ure] with a rap[idity] & noise which would have disg[usted] in any[one] else. But his mind more than redeemed it all. No man who was will[ing] to think & to be convinced & delighted, but listened with pleasure. ⟨Even⟩ The dryest legal discussions were rendered fascin[ating] even to ⟨the⟩ ladies who attended his arg[uments] in crouds & whom he was always delighted to see, & ⟨gen[erally]⟩ occas[ionally] escaped from the course of his arg[ument] to cast before them some brill[iant] imagry of the imag[ination] or rich bouquet which his fancy had formed. Having done this he returned to his arg[ument] as if it had been uninterrupted. In truth, no man has ever app[eared] at the bar of our S[upreme] C[ourt] who has furnished more lights to the Judges & rec[eived] a more undivid[ed] homage from the C[ourt] & Bar. He knew his power in arg[ument] & felt it & al[ways] sought to close the discussion & he carried This feel[ing] ⟨was carried⟩ so far as to exhib[it] an unbecoming littleness of anx[iety] at the idea of being foll[owed] by any one especially by ⟨any⟩ Webster, Wirt, Ogden & others of those strong & powerf[ul] men with whom he was associated.

But my dear F. I am tired of writing & you will be of reading what I have written & ⟨while⟩ altho I ought rather to furnish you with an example of acc[uracy] in writing, yet I am compelled ⟨to⟩ either to send this scrawl uncorrected & uncopied or leave your letter unanswered for some days to come. You must take it as it is. And in concl[usion] ⟨let me ask⟩ I ask you, how do you think P. acq[uired] his powers & his renown. In the same way that you must learn to ⟨hereafter learn to⟩ rise hereafter to em[inence] in the prof[ession] you may choose—to qualify your[self] to serve your fel[low] men & render more than happy that father & those fr[iends] who so faith[fully] disch[arge] their duty to you & who watch your progr[ess] with aching anxiety.

He had an unchast[ened] love of eminence, a perfect devotion to the acq[uisition] of knowl[edge]. ⟨& labored almost without ceasing⟩. During the day he studied while he might, at night he retired early no matter in what comp[any] he ⟨might be⟩ was found, & suff[ered] no int[erruption] but hours after mid[night] & sometimes even the dawning light found him at his labors—it is wonderful that he did not sink sooner under it, and I do believe that his—

In the margin of page 5 of the manuscript is the following:

⟨His imag[ination]⟩ I do not believe that his ⟨im[agination]⟩ ⟨fancy⟩ imag[ination] & fan[cy] was prompt ⟨or his⟩ ready. Whenever he scatters their fruits around it was manifest to a close observer that they were the result of study, & I imagine he devoted much of his time to a prep[aration] for such parts of his arg[uments] & had them always ready formed.

In the margin of page 6 are the following:

His tight cravat coat & white gloves created an unfav[orable] impr[ession] &

On lesser ⟨subjects⟩ occ[asions] his manner was more simple & to my taste much better. ⟨A few days⟩ The last time ⟨that⟩ he ⟨was⟩ spoke in the Sen[ate] he adv[ocated] a claim ⟨for⟩ of pay[ment] for the War off[ice] burned down when Mʳ. Dexter was Sec[retary] at War. He was clear, forcible & his manner simple & good.

Kind of imagination
Imag[ination]

On the verso of page 6 are the following:

In his family he was kind & affect[ionate].

I do not believe that his social feelings were of the finest & purest ⟨description⟩ order. In his family he was kind & affect[ionate], but he had ⟨great⟩ much vanity & pride & made his intercourse with the world bend to them. He required by his manners too much of attention even from those friends

and altho' he was well calc[ulated] to interest soc[iety] & himself to enjoy soc[ial] int[ercourse] when he unbent hims[elf] yet he seemed to prefer that formal inter[course] which is found among the great & seldom gave much time to his friends. This may have arisen from two causes—one his vanity which claimed precedence in attent[ion] & devotion to his books & his profession. And I imag[ine] that both were mingled & united in pro[portion] (He seldom I am told laid open his heart—he still kept something to himself he scarcely told to any.) And tho' faithf[ul] he was seldom conf[idential] in his friendships or gave much time to their cultivation.

He rec[eived] & treated grac[iously] those who yielded him precedence & first paid him their respects, but he sometimes failed to enjoy the society of Gent[lemen] of worth & who were associated

58

with him in public life & who were willing to meet on an equality [and were] too proud to yield this preced[ence] to any man.

Nothing could drive him from this course. On one occasion he was forced ⟨by the Court⟩ unprepared into ⟨the⟩ a dis[course? cussion? pute?] ⟨the room was filled with aud[itors] male & female⟩ He talked for two days, with scarcely a notice of the law & facts, but with freq[uent] & splend[id] bursts of imag[ination] ⟨& fancy⟩ totally unconnected with them, to the great delight of ⟨the⟩ his learned & unl[earned] aud[itors] male & fem[ale] of whom he had an abund[ance], but to the great annoy[ance] of the Court. At the close of the second day he was rebuked by a friend for such a waste of time & such disresp[ect] to the C[ourt]. He replied that he needed time for prep[aration], that he would be prep[ared] for the arg[ument] by the morn[ing] & he would wander no more. On the next day he delivered an arg[ument] seldom equalled, never surpassed, in which there was neither defect nor redundance.

The following passage is interlined upside down in the space left by Southard on the verso of page 6 between paragraphs 2 and 3:
I have thought that his labor was gen[erally] more connected by feeling with his own rep[utation] than with ⟨the int[erest] of⟩ a deep sense of duty to his client. To tri[umph] was too much the obj[ective]—to save his client an inferior consid[eration], but in this I may have been mistaken.

In the margins of page 7 (see reproduction) are the following:
His practice large & ought to have furnished
In Mar[yland] his name is
His death is indeed a severe loss to the fame of the ⟨whole⟩ nation for talent & ⟨will⟩ must be felt as such. To the   And altho he was less sen[sitive] than he might have been to ⟨the great⟩ imp[ortant] public int[erests] because less att[entive] to them, yet his speeches upon called const[itutional] & government ques[tions] [Deletion.] were inval[uable] to those who heard them. Of these speeches few are left by which post[erity] can judge of his talent. Either from pride or some other feeling he ⟨always⟩ prevented their public[ation] & it is prob[able] [he] has not left behind him any thing by which they may be supplied.

Samuel L. Southard and Political Patronage

THE political events of the past year—the shift in government leadership from one party to another with all the announced changes in high office and all the less well publicized turnover in lesser places—give particular piquancy to certain letters in the Samuel L. Southard Papers, letters now 120 years old but still breathing urgency as vigorously as they once did.

When Van Buren was defeated in 1840 and the Whigs were returned to power after twelve lean years of wandering in the wilderness without manna, there was an eager scramble to oust the incumbents from offices great and small and to install loyal party members. Southard was then Senator from New Jersey and early in the following year President of the Senate, and many Jerseymen looked to him anxiously as a dispenser of patronage; the volume of letters in his correspondence devoted to application for office or to recommendation of a candidate is astonishing.

To be sure, application for office was not unknown to Southard in the earlier years. There was the matter of the Assistant Doorkeeper of the Senate, a position that became available for appointment in 1837. A document in the Southard Papers defines his responsibilities, which were very gentlemanly and consisted largely of keeping the senators' desks supplied with writing materials, distributing material furnished daily by the printers to both houses as well as the more occasional bound documents, and carefully preserving them for absent senators. In these duties he had the assistance of a number of messengers "under his control," and one assumes that he was busier supervising the messengers than in carrying about "pens, ink, paper, wafers &c." There was one duty that he could not delegate, nor would he want to: in the absence of the Sergeant-at-Arms and Doorkeeper (one man), the Assistant Doorkeeper assumed his glory: he then announced messages from the President of the United States, enforced order in the Senate (no mean job in Jackson's administration), cleared the galleries when necessary, and performed various housekeeping duties for the "comfort and convenience of the Senators."

However, from the insistence of the applicants upon their need or their deserts or their mere wish to be in Washington, and from the great variety of their backgrounds, histories, and such qualifications as a few of them negligently mention, a small suspicion arises that perhaps the Assistant Doorkeeper of the Senate did not have to work very hard and just possibly drew a tidy little salary. Dr. N. C. Towle is one of my favorite candidates, though I cannot decide whether he is being delightfully frank or delightfully naïve in stating that his reason for wanting the post is that "Mrs. Towle, who is an artist and desirous as well as myself of making a collection of the portraits of the distinguished men of our country, may have the advantage of a residence in this city—by which such a design will be greatly facilitated."

Reading the letters of the many men who offered themselves as Assistant Doorkeepers, one comes to the conclusion that the coveted post must have gone to the one who most ingeniously and persuasively showed that he could gain the most profit from it, that he best knew how to exploit the opportunities latent in it, that he could make the richest use of the cultural and social fabric of Washington.

Samuel W. Thompson was equally unconcerned to make clear his ability to handle the job he sought, but he wasn't interested in cultural and social matters. "Honorable Sir," he begins, "I Rite you A few lines to Informe you that I want you to Super Sead in Gitin mc Appointed Keeper of the light House and Beacons on Sandy hook if you Will Befriend me as mutch as one hoo has Stuct to the Party throo the Manority now Wee huv Got in the majority Now I want my friends to A Sist me in Gitin that Appointment for me."

Thompson's letter is one of the deluge in 1841 pleading or demanding that Southard "A Sist" in "Gitin that Appointment." Charles Morris also had his eye on the lighthouse on Sandy Hook. He writes with more philosophy than Mr. Thompson and even with some truculence about his own position, but he also believes firmly that

> it is nesissary that there should be a change made. And as my helth is rather Delicate if you clould conveintly bestow the appointment on your humble Servent of having charge of the hook and Keeping the lights you would bestow a very great faviour. . . . You might Say (that as I have never had the pleasure of being personally acquainted with you) that you Dont Know me and as I have no reccomendation you may think I could but presented my Claims by the recomendations of Some other person claims I say as for claims I have none I dont pretend to have any claims on any office for what I can do I do Volentarily for my own wellfare as well as for my fellow citizens. I am well aware of the numerous Petetions & applications you have for offices. As I Said before if you Cannott give to me I trust you will give it to Some man in Monmouth County and with all to Some good Substancul & worthy Whig as you are well aware of the hard Tug monmouth County has had and nobly She has helped restore the Broad & Broken Seal of New Jersey. And She has given her Bastard Son his deserts withe the rest of the Bastards Sons of New Jersey & midnight office makers I wish you to remember Monmouth where Ever you can for She Stands as on a pivet. It is therefore nesisary that we all Should be Very Carefull as to our appointments to make Such as would Cause the least Bickerings in our ranks in as much as we have obtained a gloryous victory over Locofocoism we aught therefore try to keep harmony in our ranks.

The position at Barnegat Lighthouse was equally sought after. Two men, David W. Moore and James Haywood, write to Southard about it on February 27, 1841, and like Charles Morris they feel that no candidates should be considered who come from outside the district

> when competant persons can be found within it espessialy a district that has so nobly aquitted its self in the galliant Struggle for Liberty as the Township of Stafford—
> and further we consider it a bad omen for candidates to go out of their District for recommendations as none know ther qualifications so well as their own imediate Neighbours.

Sir we feel very anctious for our parts and for the cause we have so nobly tryumphed in that men of the most Sterling integrity be selected to fill all the offices within the gift of the President and his cabinet.

and after taking an impartial view of the qualifications and merrits of the applicants we decidedly give the prfferance to Jerimiah Spragg of Longbeach in Sd Township

he being in the first place what pope called the noblest work of God an Honest man—

in the second A strictly temperate man

in the third an experianced water man and we beleive those three qualifications not combined in either one of the other applicants. . . .

the loss he sustained in Cattle by the Brittish last War we are personly aquainted with, and is no hoax.

George Edwards had been before them in requesting the Barnegat Lighthouse for himself, and George Edwards had no time or thought for the Whig Party or the place whence lighthouse keepers should come; he was wholeheartedly and single-mindedly devoted to his own concerns. His letter, dated Barnegat, January 8, 1841, begins without salutation or preamble, but is well organized into three self-contained parts and eloquently written.

I take this opertunity to inform you of my Situation i am at presant aflicted with Rheumatism so that i am most descoraged of my Life for my Family is Large and all Small and dependant on my Labour for Subsistance, my ocupation Has been for 28 years Ever Sence i was able to Work for my father following the Sea by Cost wise and Know i am not able to Suport my family by that meanes no more for i have Lost my all by Sea i was one day in busyness and fin health so i thought it all ways would be Day, When i was young and my family small I hope these few Lines may find you injoying good helth and i hope your honour will please to do what you can for me in respect to that i am going to relate to you in my weak way of Expresing my self to You.

George Edwards

My motave is that by and through your honour if you plese to asist me in the apointment of the Barnegat Light House that i would Be Thankful for the apointment i am situated so that i think i Could fill the apointment and and [sic] Give Satisfaction to Every Coster that should Look for that happy Seen which i have Look for a many a Dark night Thare is a great many potitions for this same apointment and some of the potisheners never saw salt water and their under sind the same i am in hopes you will Consider that some man that has Look for Light houses before some of them was born and the remainder Lying in their beds is as well Calculated for the apointment as they with a Sound Recomendation from Captains of vesals I do hope and pray to your you will try for me if you have not pledged your self for no one Else if you will do for me I will Satisfy you as well as any other Can or will do.

I send my needy requests and humble Respects to your honour

George Edwards

I Can Git as many good Siners to my potition as any man or men would wish to See and I want you if you please to Right to me Next male day and Send me a potition of your own make for i do not no how to Compose the thing and Send it in a Letter and Send the amount for Your Trouble and i will Send you Satisfaction for your Trouble Dont forgit mee if you Please.

On the back of this letter Southard wrote that he "declined 22 Jany 1841," but nevertheless Edwards wrote again in February enclosing a petition signed by twenty-one men, seven of them captains. He also makes more explicit the "Satisfaction for your Trouble" that he was prepared to make:

And if you will will [sic] Shuv ahead for me in this apointment for me if i Should Be So Lucky as to gain the apointment these Lines may be a witness that i will Give you or what Ever Source asisists me By your Righting to me $100.00 Dollars for Your or their Servicis.

And if Nothing Can or is done for me Send Your or his Bill to me George Edwards at Barnegat and i will satesfy the Same there are 5 potitions in this neabourhood for the same apointment and only one of them are men of familes i do Expect there Aids and asistants are doing a great deal in giting the School Scollers and Bush foresters to sign their potitions i wish you to Consider that i am telling you true that my Siners are all men of Standing.

A third letter of February 16 concludes, "do not be in Doubts respecting pay for Servecse thank God i have property anough to pay that fee." As far as I can remember, this is the only bribe offered to Southard.

After these passionate and ardently persuasive letters, it is a surprise to hear the moderate and reasonable voice of Joseph Kaighn, a Quaker of Kaighns Point, New Jersey. He says that a friend, J. H. Sloan, has asked Kaighn to recommend him as "Charge des affaires to Texas, thee is acquainted with the duties appertaining to the office and likewise with Jeremiah. I throw the subject before thee, thee will act as thee thinks best." He goes on to remark that he considers the salary of the surveyor of the Port of Camden extraordinarily high and that it should be reduced by half, a comment that becomes remarkable only when we read two paragraphs later, just before he closes, that "My Son Charles informs me he has lately thought of applying for, or was willing to accept of the surveyorship of the port of Camden if there should be a new appointment made. All that I think it best for me to say to thee is that I believe his character and acquirements competent to it, and that he would be thankfull to thee for thy interest to procure it for him."

Mr. Kaighn, however, is unique among Southard's correspondents in his serene assumption that "thee will act as thee thinks best." Particularly among the applicants for postmasterships did feeling run high. After Van Buren's defeat in the election of 1840 and following "12 dark years of Toryism," John D. Hager of New Brunswick remarked that "Some of our Whig friends are as Hungry as Vultures for '*The Spoils*,'" and there was indeed a rush and scramble to oust the incumbent in appointive offices and put in a loyal Whig. Among the dozens and dozens of letters of application and recommendation it is interesting to see how seldom were the qualifications for the business of administering a post office mentioned. As Charles Morris had cogently said in his application for the Sandy Hook Lighthouse, it was all-important to put in "Some good Substancul & worthy Whig" and to be "Very Carefull as to our appointments to make Such as would Cause the least Bickerings in our ranks."

Whiggery was indeed the prime consideration, and it was generally felt that the man with the most claims upon the new administration was one who had "devoted himself knight and day to effect a change in the late administration." James Cook of Hightstown put the matter clearly: the first qualification for a candidate—party loyalty; the first reason for ousting the incumbent—he was not a good Whig. There were two candidates for the post office at Hightstown about whom Cook writes:

> ... D^r. Jonathan E. M'Chesney and D^r. Chas. C Blauvelt. I am much surprised to hear D^r. Blauvelt has made application for the Office, as he is a stranger in the place, lives intirely out of the way where the Post Office should be kept. Beside I think he has not the least claim on the Administration party, as he has been whisling about, for two or three years, ever since he has been in this place, and there was not any body knew what he belonged too. D^r. MChesney has been here many years, always a consistant undeviating wig, active as any man of the party, spending money, and time, and doing every thing in his power to promote the cause. Beside he resides in the Post Office where it has always been kept. A man much beloved by the People, much more so than his competiter. And I think would give the most Satisfaction to the Inhabitants of the Place, and the party generally. And beside he is much the best man in my humble opinion. I should like to see the saddle put on the right horse.
>
> As to myself I do not care two cents who has the office.

George Green of Belvidere says that Henry D. Swayze, "a poor man but perfectly competant and trust worthy," had been a "firm, consistant, & persevering Whig" and therefore deserved office. Isaac Watts Crane of Bridgeton describes a situation that must have been very common. "Mr Ogden the present incumbent," he wrote to Southard, "has had the office upwards of 20 years & altho he has made an excellent Post Master, falls under the rule of proscription, having at the late Presidential election, by more than a common ardour, lent his aid to the support of Vanburen & evidently shewing that his only hopes of being continued in Office depended on the election of the little Dutchman."

Of the three candidates for the post office at Bridgeton, Crane supported Edmund Davis, the hotelkeeper in the town:

> Davis says that his room back of the Front parlour which has an outer passage would make an excellent office & that it

would not at all interfere with the bar [it is not clear to me whether Mr. Crane means that the bar would not interfere with the handling of mail or vice versa], that he pays a heavy rent, that he has done as much if not more, than either of the other Gentlemen, to the advancement of the Harrison Cause— that he has always furnished Carriage & horses to accommodate the Harrison speakers & that he is not less than 50 Dollars out of pocket in his exertions to effect the late glorious triumph, that if you will vouchsafe your influence in his favour the favour will be duly appreciated. . . . I suppose you know that M^r. Davis's Daughter lately married Mr Elias P. Seeley Junr son to the late Governor Seeley & he has a Son a Graduate at Nassau Hall, now reading law with your friend L. Q. C. Elmer Esquire.

Very occasionally reference is made to conduct in office or qualifications for an office, but these remarks are generally thrown in for additional weight and are not the main burden of the argument. P. B. Shafer, who had been removed from the postmastership of Stillwater in favor of a Locofoco, righteously asks to be reinstated and says that he had performed his duties "I bleave with intier sadesfaction to the nabourhood generaley." (There was evidently no spelling requirement for postmasters.) William Van Deven's letter of recommendation contains in his argument a nice mixture of need, party loyalty, and capacity. He first speaks of his nephew, William R. Longstreet, who had emigrated to Milwaukee seven or eight years before and for a time did well in the "Mercatile Business,"

but as many Others did he entered in Speculating and the times changd and he failed, and I presume is now in Imbarised Situation. he has his mother and two Sisters to Support, beside his own famely which consist of a wife and three small children. he is an Excelent pensman and good Clerk and Business doing Man if he had means, he Informs me that he anticipates a change in the Post Office in Millwaukey, and desires your Influence in his favour in geting the Appointment.

Secondly he writes about his son, John B. Van Deven,

who has been a Soldier in the Political army for Several Campans, and has as far as his abilities was capable of Serveing has had Some hard Strugels, and faught Some hard Battles, and has at last helped to atcheve a most triumphant Victory over the Inemy of our once more Happy Land, and thinks he is Intiteled to Some of the Spoils, turn over [i. e., continued on the back]

Now my Dear Sir, I will breifly Stat to you that my Son John is Honest temperate and Industrious, and has Strove hard to Obtain an honest liveing. but he is poor, and has a Wife and Six children to Support, he has a good Inglish Education is also a good clerk. Reddy in doing business, if you cold get Some place for him he wold Ever Pray for you, and would feel Ever greatfull. I hope he May not be disappointed.

Mr. Van Deven writes with more tact than most of Southard's place-seeking correspondents; he concludes:

My Good Freind, I have no doubt but you are Over Burdened with favours of this kind, but we must be helping each other while in this world. I thus address you with much Reluctance, but the Scripture Say ask and it will be given you. Pleas grant my Request—

one of your Old Freind &c
W^m. V^n. Deven

One of the most vigorous letters was written by a man named Joseph Sharp, who writes such a firm hand and follows the lines of the folded foolscap paper so well that in spite of the peculiarities of spelling—spelling after all had not been mastered by many of Southard's correspondents—it is a surprise to read the apology in the postscript: "Sir you will Exus the Rigting of An Old Man of 81 years of Age as Cant Hardly Se what I have wrote." The letter contains so much interesting material that I will quote most of it, adding punctuation, of which it is almost wholly innocent.

Dr Sir I mak bold to wrigt you Respetting the post office at Decker Town. the present postmaster Samuel Whitekr obtained the Offis in a Manner I Call mean in the lowest Extream, had Just moved Into Deckertown. before his appointment he was at the Saim time postmaster at Unionvill, Orange County, State of New york and Continued Such for three Months or thereabouts after his Appointment At Deckertown. When at Union Vill he acted with and prfest [?] to be a Whig. on his Comeng to Deckertown he then promised on his Receiving the Appointment to Support the Loco foco party, Which he Has fulfilled to the Chalk. he Voted Ar Open ticket at our Last Election. M^r. Horas Vibber had been formerly a postmaster at Deckertown Untill he Moved to the Citi of New York when Mr Fletcher was apointed. when he, Fletcher, moved, Gran Courforr Was Appointed, Who Was Removed on accompt of his polatuks to Mak Room for Said Whitekr. When It was discovered that Corfor Was to be Remove, Horas Vibber, who had then movd back to Deckr-town, Mad application for the Offic to thos that Oficiatid. they Said that he Should have It if he woul[d] Come Over to there Side, who Replid that all the postofices in the States Could not purchas him nor Caus him to Change His prin-cipals. the postoffice has been Shamefully Conducted, it has Bean Changed from had to had [sic]. I have frquntly Called for My Papers When I have bean told there Was None, then a few owers Some time I found them In the hand of the pople in the Village; at other Times I was Dircted to Sarch for them Myself and found them in Old boxs amongst a parsel of Loos paper; at other time Time [sic] I have had other paples paper Given to Me which [I] Returd befor I Left the Town. . . . the Ofice Is Kept in a Back Room in the Store of Jonathan & John Whiteker, when the Male arives and at other Tims I have Seen the people A Rumjin of the papers without Con-trole which A Common thing.

A Store hous is In My Oponion an Improper Plais to Keep the Male. the Mail arives from the Wes throw Deckertown to Newyork and Back ivry other Day or I May Say Daley. It arives on Its Way from Avago at four a Clock in the Morning Wher the passnger Breakfast at the hous of M^r. Vibbert Who Keeps the Stand where they put Up and Chane there teams, when they have to Goe to the Store and to wak the postmaster up who live some Rods from Where the postoffice is kept in Said Store, Mr Vibber has Ben postmaster at the following Plaises to wit at Vernon. at hamburg and At Deckertown and to Kowledge Gave General Satisfacton.

therefor I solicite Your Interes In Assisting him in Geting him the said Horace Vibbert appointed postmaster at Deker-town as the Grate Wistern Mail Stops At his hous above Stated, a thing I am satisfied that Will Give Genneral Satis-faction to All partis the Whitekers Excepted.

The final sentence in Mr. Sharp's postscript is most amusing. "I forgot to Mention to You," he says, "that M^r. Horace Vibbert Is My Sone In Law." Was he compelled to make this ingenuous statement by honesty or by the feeling that he was playing a trump card? Was he a wily old fox or a forgetful old man?

Most of the letters that poured in to Southard were entirely committed to the principle of party reward for services rendered to the party, and aggressively eager to get a plum for members of their families, for friends, or for themselves. So universal was the recognition of the merits of political appointment that a man like Eli F. Cooley, Clerk of the Trustees of the College of New Jersey, who held himself above the tempest and "refused to sign *all* papers of a Political character or those any way connected with Politics," felt that he had to make clear to Southard why he had *not* signed the petition of a Mr. Burroughs, who "thinks that he has claims to the Office sought, on account of his father's services during the A. Revolution." Mr. Cooley does not support this claim, but, says he temperately, "I know not but that Mr B. would be as suitable person, as any other of our Citizens."

A father who had fought in the Revolution was almost as powerful an argument as consistent Whiggery, and next came need. Reverses in fortune, motherless children, aged parents to support—these are brought forward with great regularity. Nathaniel G. Mattison of Flemington, "a true Whig, and of the Old School of Democracy," not only has the motherless children and an old mother, but "did exibit the Farmer of North Bend, in full view in a butifull Transparency (in which I sent to Trenton for) before that long old Tavern House, that I then Occupied."

David Ball in his printed petition to the New Jersey senators and congressmen for the office of Marshal of New Jersey touches upon all the standard arguments: Revolutionary war service (once removed), financial need, and virtue, but he has grasped only half the principle of one rhetorical device and leaves the reader, though in no doubt as to what he means, as uneasy as he would be after hearing one shoe dropped.

> To the Members of the Senate, and House of Representatives of the United States, from the State of New Jersey:
>
> Gentlemen,
>
> Having petitioned the President for the Office of Marshal for the District of New Jersey, you will not, I trust, deem it

70

improper in me to lay before you some of the reasons by which I was influenced in applying for the appointment: It was not on the consideration that for thirty years I have braved the storm in my humble sphere, sparing neither time nor money in supporting those principles for which my Revolutionary Sire fought, bled, and died: that was nought but duty. Nor do I believe a plea of poverty valid; if I did, I could present you with documents showing losses within the last three years of Eighteen Thousand Dollars; but I do rely upon the fact, (if you should be satisfied, upon the all important question, "is he capable, and honest?") that for Twenty-five years past, I have served the State of New Jersey, and the United States in the capacity of Police Officer, and during this long and arduous service, I have not solicited any Office as many persons for violating the Laws of this State and the United States, as any Thirty Officers throughout the State, and that without fee or reward from this State or the United States, except the small fees for commitments.

And another consideration to my mind was, that during this long and arduous service, I have not solicited any Office from the State, or National Governments. If you can therefore consistently with your views of Justice, favor my application, it would be most thankfully received, by

Your obedient servant,
David Ball,

April 1st 1841   Newark, N.J.

Samuel C. Cook of New Brunswick can supply only a widowed mother—no ailing wife, no motherless children—but he had perhaps more powerful arguments than the display of "a butifull Transparency" to support his application for a postmastership; Jacob Edmonds lists some of them.

M^r. Cook is one of the most vigilant and influential men of our party and I think he has done much to bring about a change of Government, he is a citizen of our place, I have known him from his boyhood and if he is appointed to the office, it will be very gratifying to a large majority of our citizens, there was a call made for a public meeting in this city signed by about one hundred of our most respectable citizens the meeting was a large one and they almost unanimously requested that M^r. Cook should be our postmaster.

But Cook's own letter gives such a clear picture of the situation at New Brunswick, speaks so interestingly of Southard, and withal concludes with such a splendid burst of rhetoric, that it must be quoted in full.

New Brunswick 6 March 1841

To the Hon S L Southard

D Sir Alto a Strange to you personally I hope you will not object to one who Claimes himself a Jerseyman to address you as I do it without consultation with any of my friends. I am a candidate for the Post Office in this City and shall forward to the Post Master General next week my petition for that office and it will be signed by a majority of the *Whig* Voters of this City & Vacinity. It is said here by some that the Matter is all arainged and that you have pledged your influence to M^r. Snowdon who is the Brother in law of the Messrs Randolph in reply to this assertion of the friends of M^r. S. I have said that it could not be as in all your official life you have proved yourself to be a Democrat of the old Scholl and therefore you would be governed by the will of the people in your selection of men whom you would recomend or support for office. I will state to you my course in this Matter A few days after the Election of Gen Harrison was known here M^r. Snowdon Called on me saying that he had heard I was a Candidate for the P. O. I replyed in the affirmative and remarked to M^r. S. that we had Just gone through a very exciting an Election and begged him that we should not get up another now for the offices but as far as him & Myself was concerned that we might refer it to our mutual Friends the leaders of the Party or to a public meeting of the Party both of which proposition he rejected the excitement continued & rather increased by M^r. S. Petition being put in Circulation in different parts of the City. I then Called on Judge Booraem our County Clerk who thought I could do nothing else to prevent a Number of Candidates from offering themselv[es] and increasing the dificulty but to Call a public Meeting which mode was suggested to a number of friends of the various candidates which at this time amounted to about six the call was made out and signed by friends of 'l the Candidates. M^r. S. Friends declined attending the meeting the result of that meeting satisfyed I believe all the candidates that I was the choice of the whigs of this City for P M I will now say one word about myself and Family and ask from you as one of the representative of N Jersey Your assistance in this matter so far as you may act for me in this you will receive the Gratitude of one who needs your assistance. I am the Grand Son of Capt Guain McCoy of Baskenridge. I have a widowed Mother depending on me for Support that Mother was born and braught up in the same place with Yourself was one who went to the same scholl one who was intimate with and your playmate in the days of your Childhood one whose Farther as you know faught for the liberties that we now enjoy that Mother is poor in health and poor so far as this worlds goods are concerned that Mother now asks one of her playmates in Childhood to assist her in her declining days.

Your Ob^t Servt

S. C. Cook

Was Southard's heart moved by the thought of Captain McCoy's daughter, his playmate in the days of happy childhood at Baskingridge? Did he even remember her? Even if he did, I rather think that the hundred names signed to the petition for a meeting to support Mr. Cook's candidacy would have had greater weight with him than a sentimental recollection. The ways of man are capricious, to be sure, and his reasons for a given decision often cloudy even to himself, but in 1841, with thousands of office-hungry Whigs clamoring for satisfaction, it is at least likely that Southard gave his support to the man whose appointment would create around him the largest possible island of Whig contentment.

What the other considerations were that influenced him we get a little glimpse of from a few pages of brief notes, headed respectively "Memo: of cases, designed for a conversation with M^r. Curtis," "Short memo: of Cases, in which M^r. Southard feels some interest, & to which he asks the attention of M^r. Curtis, before an adverse decision may be made," and "Appointments desired by me," which give us some clue to his attitude.

On the subject of service in the war for independence as a qualification: "John De Camp—Inspector of Metals. A *revolutionary* man—a friend of my father. He is old. If *too old* I have nothing to say. I am informed that he has been—thus far— *honest, skilful,* faithful. Why not spare him?"

On need: Southard lists three applicants for the lighthouse at the "Highlands of Neversink"; of one he concludes, "If he has the skill, he is most worthy"; of another that the Whigs do not much favor him; and of the third, "For him I have most *sympathy*. His father Jos. Doty, was, for some years, Keeper there—faithful & worthy. He was dismissed to make room for the late Keeper—& *solely* on account of his political opinions. He has left a family, widow & children, which the applicant has to support. He is an intelligent & excellent young man, but whether he has the skill, I cannot, at this time, answer."

On Whig loyalty: "Is competent & has good wishes of the Whigs of Warren, Morris &c &c. *Against* every member of his family, he has been true." "Good Whig & worthy of place in Cus. House." "In all respects worthy, & his app^t. would be great kindness to some of the best & most influential people of our State." "He is, as *I believe*, an honest man—a competent—& a Whig. *Save him.*"

It is notable, I think, that Southard always mentions the competence of the applicant as well as his loyalty to the party. The clearest expression of his feeling is to be found in a little scrap of paper, twice folded and written in pencil, a note made at a conference, perhaps, and tucked into an envelope of notes on cases. It says: "Republican Gratitude. Its best exhibition is in doing justice—not in bestowing office without reference to qualifications."